The International Library of Sociology

THE STUDY OF GROUPS

Founded by KARL MANNHEIM

The International Library of Sociology

THE SOCIOLOGY OF THE SOVIET UNION
In 8 Volumes

THE STUDY OF GROUPS

by

JOSEPHINE KLEIN

First published in 1956 by
Routledge

Routledge is an imprint of the Taylor & Francis Group

Reprinted in 1998, 2002
by Routledge

2 Park Square, Milton Park, Abingdon, Oxon, OX14 4RN

Transferred to Digital Printing 2007

British Library Cataloguing in Publication Data
A CIP catalogue record for this book
is available from the British Library

The Study of Groups
ISBN 0-415-17798-7
The Sociology of Behaviour and Psychology: 18 Volumes
ISBN 0-415-17834-7
The International Library of Sociology: 274 Volumes
ISBN 0-415-17838-X

Publisher's Note
The publisher has gone to great lengths to ensure the quality of this reprint
but points out that some imperfections in the original may be apparent

Contents

CONTENTS

vii

Acknowledgements

The main debts I have to acknowledge are those I owe to the writers listed in the Bibliography at the back. Two names may be singled out: that of R. F. Bales and that of G. C. Homans. To Professor Homans I owe thanks not only for an intellectual debt, but also for help and encouragement over a period of years.

I owe much to the kindness and wisdom of Mr. E. F. Piercy, formerly in charge of the Research Section of the National Association of Boys' Clubs, who first drew my attention to the need for the study of small groups.

In addition, I am deeply indebted to my friends in the Faculty of Commerce and Social Science in the University of Birmingham, in particular Michael Beesley and F. H. Hahn, whose contributions and suggestions were too numerous for footnotes, and my former colleague, G. Duncan Mitchell, who has been invaluable in matters of presentation and style.

I am glad of the opportunity to thank again the students who served as guinea-pigs for the study described in the Appendix, and the secretarial staff of the Faculty, who with exquisite patience typed and retyped the manuscript.

Birmingham, 1955.   J.K.

CHAPTER ONE

The Performance of Tasks in Groups

THIS book is intended to acquaint the reader with the material which other workers have accumulated in the field of small group studies. The material is arranged in the hope that in the course of the analysis, as chapter succeeds chapter, a fairly general theory of social life will gradually take shape. Social life is very complex, so complex that it eludes analysis—but it is also so fascinating that it presents a constant challenge to the mind. We have tried to respond to this challenge in the following way. As we see it, analysis requires the isolation of important variables and a description of the effect these variables exercise upon one another. Fortunately or unfortunately, social life presents a situation in which all variables —we don't know which they are and we don't know how many—react upon one another to an unknown extent. We are thus faced with two difficulties: that of identifying what can usefully be regarded as important variables, and that of finding a starting point at which to break into the circle of their interaction, when we try to describe them.

We shall minimise the first difficulty by narrowing our field and thus reducing the number of aspects that have to be described. When one narrows the field one takes into account only a few variables and assumes that if other variables exist, they remain constant, that is to say, they do not produce changes in the situation that is being considered. In the study of small groups, for instance, the culture of the society and the personality of group members are among the conveniently disregarded aspects.

Our second difficulty—where to break into the circle—we solve as far as we can in the same way. We start with a very simple situation, with two or three variables in interaction, and consider the effect they would have upon one another *if no other variables were to affect the situation.* Thus in the present chapter we assume at first that the task which the members are to perform is a very simple one, and that all members are equal in strength and skill. Then we ask ourselves how our conclusions would have to be modified if members differed in strength or skill; and then we qualify our new conclusions by assuming that the task is a complicated one. Such an approach makes of course very often for grossly unrealistic assumptions and findings, but by gradually adding to the number of variables under consideration, one may hope to approximate the 'model' more and more to social life as we know it.

For this reason, the reader may at times be irritated, especially in the earlier chapters, by statements that he considers too general, or by the omission of what seem to him obvious considerations. I hope that he will find such generalisations qualified later in the book as new considerations are brought into the discussion. In the present chapter, for instance, we shall discuss the principles underlying differences in the efficiency with which groups of various sizes perform different kinds of tasks. Yet we do not take account of the fact that members may compete with one another, or that there may be difficulties in communication, or differences in organisation, although these are important and relevant considerations. But the complexity of social life may be our excuse for introducing these factors at a later stage in the argument.

Our problems in the present chapter are such as these: when is it worth while to form a group in order to solve a problem? When does a group perform a task more efficiently than an individual? When is a larger group more efficient than a smaller one? Let us therefore consider what we imply when we use the word 'efficient'.

Generally efficiency is measured in terms of speed of solution, or accuracy of solution, or both. But when we refer to the speed with which a solution is reached by individual or group, we may find ourselves thinking of time in two senses. If one person performs a task in five hours and three persons perform the task in three hours' co-operation, how justified are we in saying that the second method 'took less time'? For in terms of man-hours, the first solution took five, and the second three times three, or nine, hours. Husband (1940) has shown that while for certain tasks like decoding and jig-saw puzzles individual workers take more time than do pairs of workers co-operating, the pairs never worked for less than two-thirds of the period required by solitary subjects. Only if they had taken half the time would the total expenditure of time have been equivalent in the two cases. Was co-operation an 'efficient' way of performing this task?

We will now try to describe more precisely in what circumstances it will be worth while to form a group.

ASSUMPTION ONE

The members of the group are equal in strength or skill, and the task they perform is very simple.

As a prototype of this, the very simplest conception of a group member's contribution to a task, one may take a study by Moede (1927) of the increased strength of the group as more members add their weight. The members of the group were required to pull a rope as hard as they could. The strength of pull could be measured in pounds. At intervals another man was added to the group. The addition of another man increased the power of the group, but it decreased the average contribution made by the members. That is to say, with each addition in group membership, the effect of each man's effort was lessened. The decrease in average contribution becomes more and more marked, as the following table will show.

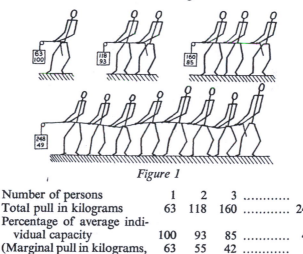

Figure 1

Number of persons	1	2	3	....	8
Total pull in kilograms	63	118	160	....	248
Percentage of average individual capacity	100	93	85	....	49
(Marginal pull in kilograms,	63	55	42	....	–

This series is analogous to that of average and total product in

3

economics; in both cases the marginal contributions—the addition to the total product that is due to the addition of one more contribution—is of particular interest. One does not arrive at the total strength of the group by adding the individual 'strengths' of members. Each man's contribution is a marginal one. Thus, the effect of co-operation in the performance of a task is interactive, that is to say, the group product is the result not only of the strength of each member, but also a result of the effect that each member's effort has on the efforts of other members.

Gordon (1924), in a different kind of task, asked subjects to estimate the weights of a series of objects. These subjects did not meet, i.e. there was no interaction between them. She then formed artificial aggregates of various sizes by grouping the reply slips of paper, and found that the larger the groupings the more closely the averaged estimated rankings correspond to the actual rankings of weights. The reason is plainly that errors tend to cancel one another in accordance with statistical laws; they do so more completely as the number of estimates increases. In this situation the 'group' existed only in so far as the experimenter made the 'members' interact in her own mind. The experimenter is a 'member of the group' by virtue of her co-ordinating activity.[1]

Watson (1928), by using Gordon's technique, was able to show that interaction between members may have an adverse effect on the total output of a number of persons. His subjects had the task of constructing anagrams, i.e. of building words from given letters. He found that groups do better than individuals working alone. But when he constituted himself the sole co-ordinator and repeated Gordon's procedure with those of his subjects who had worked alone, combining the answers and discarding duplicate words, he found that this aggregate had done better than the actual groups in interaction. This, on the level of simple intellectual tasks, is similar to Moede's result. The difference is that Moede's subjects must have

---

[1] Errors will, of course, only cancel by this process when there is no cultural or other bias affecting all individuals in the same direction. When there is no objective criterion of validity, for instance in aesthetic judgement, averaged estimates will do no more than reflect the attitude prevailing in the culture. Thus Stroop (1932) asked subjects to rank pictures of oriental rugs in order of their beauty. She found that each rug was rated among the three most beautiful by some members and among the three least beautiful by some other members. There was no general agreement, even though with the larger group, agreement (defined in a statistical sense) was somewhat greater than in the smaller groupings.

4

got in each other's way, whereas Watson's subjects distracted one another because they did not confine themselves to the task but took time off to enjoy each other's company. In this connection it is interesting to note that South (1927) and Gurnee (1937) both found that single-sex committees are more efficient than mixed ones! The group provides distraction and this is bound to show in the result. We may anticipate a later discussion by pointing out that such a group effect is not necessarily inefficient where task performance is concerned. The disadvantages of interaction between group members are only important when the task is simple, the goal unimportant to the members and the duration of the group so short that the problem of keeping members happy need not arise. When these conditions do not obtain, the presence of other members will reinforce positive and compensate for negative aspects of the task. Then the effort not devoted to work may serve a morale-building function. But this is outside the scope of the present chapter.[1]

We conclude, therefore, that where the task is simple and members equal in strength or skill, the task will be performed more quickly and more accurately if there is no interaction between the members except insofar as they are organised by an 'entrepreneur' with whom they all interact and who works out the final solution. The disadvantages of this type of organisation are discussed in a later chapter.[2]

ASSUMPTION TWO

Let us now assume an unequal degree of skill among the members.

Consider an experiment by South (1927) who set groups of three and of six members to solve a problem involving a simple mechanical construction—what combination of manipulations made a bell ring. The problem was solved when all members agreed that a solution was correct. When the solution had been found, the bell could be made to ring at will. The larger groups tended to solve this problem very much more rapidly than the smaller. The reason for this is not hard to find. Plainly a solution depends on the insight and skill of one member of the group who happens, through experience or natural aptitude, to be particularly skilled at problems of this nature. The more people there are in the group, the more likely it is to con-

[1] But see pages 99–104.   [2] See pages 57–63.

5

tain an expert member, and the higher is the probability of a speedy solution.

What is happening here reminds one of Allee's findings on goldfish (1939). When one of his goldfish was conditioned to find his way out of an aquarium maze and then put among untrained fish, the rate of learning of such a group was higher than that of a complete group of untrained fish. Once one member of the group has the correct solution, the others can follow his lead.

This may be amplified by yet another experiment. Bekhterev and de Lange (1924) presented subjects with stimuli to which they were expected to respond in an imaginative way. They were, for instance, confronted with a pair of pictures and required to state all the resemblances they could think of, continuing this process until they had no more to say. Here again groups do better than individuals. The experimenters attribute this to a tendency on the part of the group to bring out 'hidden resemblances', but it is more likely that the result was due to what one might call a series of landslides. When the group showed signs of flagging, someone would introduce a quite new angle, such as remarking on the colours of the pictures, whereupon an avalanche of new contributions would be made on the same lines by other members until, this also flagging, the process was repeated with a new dimension again, such as perhaps the family relationships involved.

Therefore, when there are differences in skill and each man has to reach a solution, interaction between the members of a group will enable the less skilled members to solve the problem because of the help they receive from more skilled members. In these circumstances it is worth while to form a group. The presence of the expert will produce a solution to benefit the whole group. And plainly, the larger the group, the more likely is the chance inclusion of an expert. This generalisation will only hold, however, in the conditions stated: (1) the degree of skill must be unequally divided among members, and (2) the problem must have a solution which can be verified by all.

ASSUMPTION THREE

Let the correct solution be unverifiable.

Gordon showed that, in accordance with statistical laws, the larger the aggregate the more correct the averaged answers, when a question of fact is at stake, such as the weight of an object. Similarly,

6

South's mechanical problem discussed above was a factual and verifiable one. Members were convinced that the solution was correct by the fact that the bell rang. The larger the group, the sooner the problem was solved. Where the solution is not immediately obvious, or where there is not one single solution which is the correct one, the very reverse of this generalisation holds true. Thus South finds that in judging the emotion portrayed in a series of photographs, the smaller group came to a unanimous decision more quickly than the the larger. The reason for this must be obvious. Here was no truth which became self-evident once it had been demonstrated. Each member had to be separately convinced by argument. The more members there are the longer this is likely to take[1].

To sum up our argument so far, the presence of an expert in a group will improve the performance of less skilled members if the problem is such that the expert solution can be recognised as correct. If the correct solution cannot be so easily recognised, the group spends a long time arguing the merits of different solutions.

A light is thus thrown on the place of the expert in the group. We have noted that the group tends to distract the individual from his best performance. Now we see that if the expert is right, but not manifestly so, he is held back because he has to persuade others. If he is manifestly right, the group will accept his judgement, but then we may ask why a group was needed at all. One answer is that the expert's decisions have to be carried out by others who will feel more responsible for the successful execution of the scheme if they have participated in making the decision or solving the problem. The expert must therefore have skill in human relations as well as in his own field if he is to function usefully in a group where other members are less skilled than he is. Where, for instance, a policy advocated by an expert has to be accepted by an executive committee, and the expert is better qualified to decide than the committee is,

---

[1] Speed of problem solving will vary inversely with the size of the group not only when there is properly speaking no solution, but also in such problems as, for instance, the construction of crossword puzzles, whose solution requires the simultaneous consideration of so many factors that an allotment of tasks is necessary if any course of action is to be consistently pursued (Thorndike, 1938). McCurdy and Lambert's groups of three, for example (1952), were required to solve a mechanical construction problem infinitely more complicated than South's. The members might still have been more efficient than individuals working alone had they been able to organise themselves so that each member would play a special role—recording unsuccessful solutions, determining the order in which members might contribute, and so on. As it was, the members interfered with one another and the groups proved inefficient.

techniques can be used to guide the discussion in such a way that the members may arrive at the same conclusion as the expert and yet feel that they have contributed a good deal.

Such a technique has been evolved by Maier (1950). He argues that a man may pursue his own line of thought longer than is useful unless he can be made to review the problem as a whole. Interaction in a group tests and stimulates a man's thinking.

'Ideas are constantly suggested by chance events, by the remarks of others, and by the things we look at. However, the ideas that are used or selected depend on our direction (of thought). Thus, one failure to solve our problems is due to our inability to react to suggestions when we have a false or fruitless direction. Such directions are far worse than none at all, and this is one of the reasons why many problems are solved when we are engaged in recreational activities, or when we make fresh starts. The direction in thinking has momentum and tends to perpetuate itself. If we are to influence or aid the thinking of others, this can more readily be achieved by recognising and influencing the direction their thinking is taking. A given idea is plausible only when it is consistent with a direction. Since one approach is likely to be more fruitful than another on a given problem, much depends on the direction the thinking takes.'

For this reason Maier advocates that the expert should have skill to minimise the tendency to persevere on an unfruitful or narrow approach. The expert does so by facilitating good communication between the members. A trained leader would guide discussion on the following lines:

'Do not present the group with the problem but instead determine from the group whether they have a problem.

Recognise all suggestions but influence direction in thinking by asking for further suggestions.

Protect individuals from criticism of other group members by interpreting all remarks in a favourable light.

Make a list of all suggestions so that all types of considerations are included.

When the list is fairly complete, probing questions may be asked, e.g. 'how can we change things so as to combine some of these features?'

Good suggestions may be kept in the discussion by asking 'how would that work out', etc.

Do not hasten the solution by capitalising on the first good lead or in any other way reflect your preferences.

Always work toward the ideal of removing undesirable features from the job. Make your objective one of resolving differences in the group.'

By this means the expert not only gives group members the conviction that the decision is theirs and theirs therefore the responsibility of making it succeed, he is also able to test his own ideas out against those of the rest of the group and he himself may change his ideas as the result of the discussion that took place. This leads us directly to another aspect of our argument: a problem may be so complicated that more than one expert is needed to solve it.[1]

ASSUMPTION FOUR

Let the problem to be solved consist of a series of sub-problems.

In the study by Watson already quoted, the group produced a solution which was superior to that of the best member working alone. It is therefore to be supposed that the group has in some cases a good effect on the expert. The help that is afforded him is of two kinds: directly constructive and critical. When a problem can be broken down into a number of slighter problems which have to be worked out consecutively, not all these minor solutions need necessarily come from the member we have termed the expert. One needs in effect a series of little experts in many cases. Moreover, Thorndike's experience with groups solving crossword puzzles (1928) shows that one member's suggestions, even when not correct, may act as a trigger to the correct responses of others. The group is then not only more efficient, but *cumulatively* more so than the individual.

Shaw (1938), whose groups of four were given tasks each step of which had to be solved before the next one could satisfactorily be tackled, confirms this finding. She finds, moreover, that members who do not advance solutions may yet by their criticisms give grounds for discarding incorrect suggestions and thus lessen the time spent on solving the problem. An increase in the size of the group therefore not only enlarges the field from which possible solutions

[1] See the discussion also pages 16–19.

9

may be forthcoming, but also that from which necessary criticism may emerge. This is of particular interest since most of the problems that committees have to deal with are of this complex character. Members of the group not only add to the body of knowledge and ingenuity at the disposal of the group, they play a vital role as critics and discarders of false theories. It may therefore be suggested that many groups consist of members each of whom is an expert in his own way. Each member has a special skill to contribute to the group and contributes in his own way to the survival of that group. A natural division of function comes about in this way. It is to this problem that the next chapter is devoted.

*

We sum up our findings in a number of simple generalisations.

(1) Speed in problem-solving may be calculated either in hours or in man-hours.

(2) The contribution made by a member to the group, when all members are equally skilled, must be seen in terms of the marginal rather than the average contribution.

(3) The composite result of individuals working singly is better than the group product; larger aggregates cancel errors more efficiently than smaller in accordance with statistical theory, provided:

(a) an objective assessment is possible (e.g. this does not apply to aesthetic opinions).

(b) the problem is a single step one.

(c) the task is short and interesting to members.

(d) unanimity of opinion is of no importance.

(4) Where the problem to be solved has only one correct answer which can be verified at once:

(a) the speed with which a unanimous solution appears varies directly with the degree of skill of the most skilled member.

(b) since the probability that the group contains a highly skilled member varies directly with the size of the group, the speed with which a solution appears varies directly with the size of the group.

(c) when the problem is very complicated and a division of function evolves, these propositions do not hold.

(5) Where the problem to be solved has only one correct answer, which can be verified, but which has to be reached through several steps of argument, propositions 4(a) and 4(b) hold. In addition, another factor must be considered:

(d) several skills may be involved and these may be contributed by different members of the group.

(6) We identify three types of efficient contributions which members may make:

(a) correct suggestions.
(b) correct criticisms.
(c) 'trigger' suggestions.

(7) Where a problem to be solved has a correct solution which cannot be verified by the group:

(a) accuracy increases with size of group since errors tend to cancel each other.
(b) accuracy increases with a higher average level of skill in the group.
(c) unanimous agreement that a solution has been reached will be difficult.

(8) Where a problem to be solved has no correct and verifiable answer, the speed with which a conclusion is reached varies inversely to the size of the groups.

CHAPTER TWO

Differentiation in the Group: (1) Functional Authority

IN the present chapter we build on what has gone before and add two further complications. The first of these arises from the fact that during the life of the group there emerge differences between the functions of individual members. This was foreshadowed when we discussed the solution of complicated problems in the previous chapter. There may be a number of 'experts' in the group. When their expertise becomes recognised other members will willingly look to them for advice and guidance. In this way, they will perform a kind of leadership function. The second complication we introduce in this chapter relates to this leadership function. We shall be concerned with the manner in which different group members can induce others to be led by them. We shall call it leadership and we shall define it as *the ability to elicit from others the response they desire.*

The ability to elicit from others a desired response is an essential component of the definition of such concepts as 'power', 'leadership', 'status', 'control', 'influence', 'authority', 'dominance'. These words refer to different ways or different contexts in which the ability to elicit such a response is exercised. We shall examine this ability in three kinds of groups and call it force, functional authority and status authority respectively. The three kinds of groups are the following: (1) the group in which differentiation between members is based on the overt use of force, or the threat of it; (2) groups that are differentiated according to functional authority, in which we shall see authority arising from the nature of the task and vested, by implication, in the man who is recognised as best able to perform that task; and (3) groups differentiated by status authority, where one man exercises authority permanently, more or less regardless of

12

the situation of the group. This last case is discussed at length in the next chapter.[1]

Differentiation among members of the group based on the overt use of force is found only in certain unusual conditions which are best typified by instances from the animal kingdom. C. Murchison (1934–5), for instance, in his studies of groups of six chickens shows that a perfectly linear hierarchy of dominance becomes stable and permanent when the chicks are about thirty-six weeks old. Dominance shows itself in four ways: energy in establishing contacts, ability to defeat others in combat, sexual prowess, and the extent to which favourable reactions are elicited from the opposite and unfavourable reactions from chickens of the same sex. From nine months on, chick A will dominate the five other chicks in all these ways, B will dominate four and be dominated by A, C will dominate three and be dominated by A and B, and so on.[2]

Chickens dominated	Chickens dominating					
	YY	Blue	G	R	W	Y
YY	–	0	0	0	0	0
Blue	1	–	0	0	0	0
G	1	1	–	0	0	0
R	1	1	1	–	0	0
W	1	1	1	1	–	0
Y	1	1	1	1	1	–

Figure 1

YY → Blue → G → R → W → Y

Figure 2

Such perfect linearity in structure is largely attributable to the extreme simplicity of the organisms concerned, in that variables such as learning, organisation of work, etc., are excluded by the experi-

[1] Popularity also enables a man to elicit a desired response, but he does not have to accredit it as though it were a skill and he an expert.

[2] When a strange chicken enters the group after the hierarchy has been established in this way, he is subject to attack by all the others. Schjelderup-Ebbe (Pecking order in hens, reported in Murchison, 1934–5, and also in Murchison, *Handbook of Social Psychology*, 1935), from whom Murchison derived much of his work, postulates that these attacks serve the function of establishing the newcomer's proper position in the hierarchy. They are therefore a sort of exploratory behaviour. He supports his theory by showing that in the very young, where these hierarchies are not as yet firmly established, there is no discrimination between newcomers and others. Although we discuss here only structure based on dominance, this particular result seems capable of further generalisation.

menter's choice of subjects. When we come to creatures higher in the evolutionary scale, to the chimpanzees, difficulties in the method of describing structure solely in terms of dominance and submission begin to show themselves. Companionship preferences, apparently closely related to grooming activities—the more efficient being preferred—must be taken into consideration. Moreover, the hierarchy based on aggressive dominance no longer relates perfectly to this preference structure, and dominance itself, tested in two different ways, does not yield identical results (Nowlis, 1939).

With immature human beings, permanent and linear hierarchies are still more rarely observed. While in children's studies evidence can be found that some children are consistently obeyed either directly or implicitly by imitation in many different kinds of activity and circumstance, these leaders already begin to show a certain specificity, some being acknowledged leaders in one sphere, and others in others (N. Polansky, R. Lippitt, F. Redl, 1950). Merei (1949), studying children in a day nursery, detects individual differences in the means by which they manage to get their own way. We find 'order-givers', 'proprietors', 'diplomats', and others. All the same, there is a line to be drawn between leaders and followers, as is shown by Hanfman's (1938) interesting finding that though different children may be leaders in different situations—a corollary of Merei's findings—the followers are always followers; they follow any leader. There is then a situation in which A will dominate B on one occasion, and B dominate C, while at other times C might dominate A and B. But among the followers the hierarchy is permanent and indifferent to changes of activity.

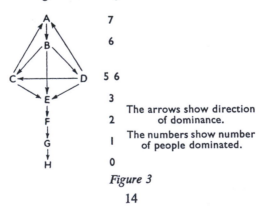

The arrows show direction of dominance.

The numbers show number of people dominated.

Figure 3

14

This diagram shows also how dominance begins to be less in terms of individuals and more in terms of leading sub-groups or élites. A, B, C and D between them must control pretty nearly all the group behaviour of those lower down the scale.

Whyte (1943) shows a similar structure in a gang of late adolescents, with Doc, Mike and Danny near the top and other members submitting to their leadership.

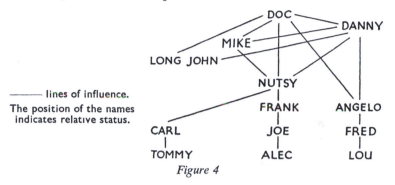

lines of influence.
The position of the names indicates relative status.

Figure 4

At an earlier stage leadership was more definitely hierarchical. Doc's account of how he became the leader is remarkably reminiscent of the way pecking order is established among Murchison's hens:

'Nutsy was the head of our gang once. I was his lieutenant. He was bigger than me and had walloped me different times before I finally walloped him. When he walloped me, there weren't many people around, so I didn't mind, but the one time he broke his promise that he wouldn't hit me, there was a big crowd around. I was a proud kid. I couldn't let him get away with that. . . . You see, I was wrestling him, and I had him down. "If I let you up," I said, "will you promise not to hit me?" He promised, but when I let him up and turned away, he cracked me on the nose, and I got a bloody nose. I went after him and was beating him up when the big fellows stopped us. . . . Next day I saw him leaning against the wall. I went up to him and said, "I'll kill you," and let him have one. He didn't fight back. He knew I was his master. So after that I was the leader, and he was my lieutenant. . . . That was when I was thirteen or fourteen. . . . Nutsy was a cocky kid before I beat him up. . . . After that, he seemed to lose his pride. I would talk to him and try to get him to buck up. . . . After I walloped him, I told

15

the boys what to do. . . . If they didn't, I walloped them. I walloped every kid in my gang at some time. . . .'

Our general conclusion so far must be that linear hierarchies based on overt dominance become more rare as members of groups become capable of a greater variety of activities, and as each member of the group develops his own distinctive skills. Our problem will be to identify some of the factors which determine the differentiation of adult groups.

Differentiation in the group implies that there are differences between members perceived by the members themselves, often differences which are respected and maintained by them. Although we shall later work with different assumptions, at present we assume that differences in the group exist only in so far as the group brings them into existence, permits them to exist, one might almost say 'invents' them.

Differentiation does not necessarily presuppose a ranking order, although the two are frequently found together. Thus Homans' definition of rank—'the evaluation of a man relative to the evaluation of other members of the group'—is equally suitable as a definition of differentiation (Homans, 1950, p. 140). It is possible to conceive of differentiation in a group in which no ranking is possible, all members being considered equally valuable.

By the exercise of a man's skill, by virtue of his function in the group, a man may be able to elicit the response he desires from others. The exercise of skill can give a man the right to lead others for as long as that skill is being used by the group. When other skills are called for, others will lead the group. In brief, skill may give a man authority. There are, however, so many factors making for the divorce of leadership from specific skills that this type of group is relatively rarely met with.[1] Nevertheless, all spontaneously formed groups, that is, groups whose structure is not determined by an experimenting sociologist or some other agency, do pass through a phase similar to the one to be described below.

The generalisations in this section are valid only in so far as the following assumptions hold:

[1] In more sociological language, initially status is 'achieved' but there are factors, to be discussed in detail in the next chapter, which operate in such a way as to shift the status more and more to an 'ascribed' position. It is also interesting to note that simultaneously status ceases to be 'specific' and becomes 'diffuse'.

16

(1) The personality of members is such that they do not like to be dominated by force; all members are capable of many kinds of activity and interaction.

(2) The group and its structure is not externally determined; members may freely communicate with each other and are free to leave the group when they wish. It is by virtue of this assumption that the findings here contrast with those of later chapters.

(3) The group has to perform either a very complicated task or more than one task. It has therefore also a certain duration. This assumption will not greatly restrict the generality of our propositions since almost all adult groups are in some sense task-groups. They come together for the achievement of a certain purpose. Even where this is not explicitly so, as in a group of friends, the problems of maintaining good internal relations and good relations between the group and its environment remain.

(4) The group deals mainly with 'fully-fledged' problems. The concept of the fully-fledged problem was first used by Bales (1951) in order to single out a type of problem-solving group for which his own generalisations would hold. He stipulates that members of the group must between them be in possession of all the facts needed to reach a decision or solve a problem, but that no member should possess all the facts. (We shall see that in an enduring group this condition is in fact one which tends always to obtain since different members have access to different parts of the environment.) Further, but less important in the present context, members should have somewhat different value-preferences, and more than one decision may with equal justification be made. The assumption that the problem is a fully-fledged one ensures that all members are needed to take part in the group activities, if the task is to be well performed.

(5) The behaviour of members shall be rational, in the sense that information suggesting a certain course of action shall in fact dictate that course of action. Leadership (here defined as the ability to elicit a desired response with the willing co-operation of the other) will therefore inhere in that member who knows most about a particular problem as long as that problem is the one most urgently requiring solution. When, therefore, we speak

C 17

of an order-giving hierarchy, it will be exactly the same as an information-giving hierarchy, for the decision-making power will be distributed in proportion to the amount that any member knows about the problem in hand.[1]

By virtue of these assumptions we discard from our consideration all groups in which differentiation is attained by the use of force. Instead, we consider groups in which differentiation is directly and exclusively brought about by differences in skill in solving the problems which confront the group and which may threaten its survival. Where leadership is equated with the exercise of skill, it is possible for a simple hierarchy to develop in which the more skilled communicate orders to the less skilled, provided the task is simple and requires the exercise of only one skill. When, however, a task is so complicated that different skills are needed at different stages, there is no *a priori* reason for supposing that excellence in all these skills will be vested in the same person. Therefore, the order-giving hierarchy (which is also the information-giving one, and, more generally the communication-network) will shift with the requirements of the group. If the problem is a fully-fledged one, every member of the group will at some time be giving information (or orders) to the other members of the group. In these circumstances it is impossible to identify any kind of permanent hierarchical differentiation.

Even when one member initially possesses all the skills to solve a problem, there will be many shifts of control in the groups if other members are required to carry out the task. If this is the case, an interesting situation arises. Whenever tasks are carried out by persons other than the leader, the members come to possess information to which the leader has no access except through them, for example, information concerning the reaction of outsiders or the intractability of materials. If problem-solving and the performance of tasks, and not the maintenance of high status by certain members, are indeed

[1] This may strike the reader as an unusual assumption but it is a useful one. In a later chapter we shall assume that group networks determine the flow of information. If, however, we assume that information exercises a certain constraining influence on members, i.e. that the possession of information gives control, we shall find that any network carries with it implications about the status of certain members (or certain positions in the network). Where all members have similar positions and similar access to resources (information or skills) differences in status cannot become permanent. Where certain positions favour the acquisition of information, status differences become permanent much more easily. See page 47 and also pages 137–40.

the main ends of the group, then again the information-giving function (and correct information implies the freedom to give orders) will be distributed over all the members of the group. Each member will be playing his distinctive indispensable part in the group and it is impossible to evaluate members in terms of higher and lower status. But though status distinctions may be irrelevant, differentiation of function may be clearly marked. Instead of examining the group for leadership-structure, it then becomes important to examine the task for its functional components.

Mary Parker Follett's ideas are so relevant to this discussion and her expression of them so pungent that a brief summary of them may be justified. Her starting point is the increased specialisation of our times: we have evolved a society of experts. One willingly submits to the advice of one's dentist or one's plumber, because of one's trust in their superior knowledge. Authority inheres in the good performance of a task. 'People often talk about the limit of authority when it would be better to speak of the definition of the task.' The man who seeks to become a leader is advised: 'forget your personality and learn your job'. She assumes, not always altogether justifiably, that in any situation there is one way of doing a piece of work and that is the best way. This means that the rules of operation arise naturally out of the task and cannot satisfactorily be laid down by anyone who is not himself an acknowledged expert in the work. Groups of people work best when they know themselves to be skilled in recognising the requirements—almost the logic—of the situation. If they can do this, other personality differences are irrelevant to the organisation of the work.

'It is by an understanding of the laws which govern the process by which authority is generated that we gain our freedom . . . in any true sense of the word. For authority is the outcome of our common life. It does not come from separating people, from dividing them into two classes, those who command and those who obey. It comes from an intermingling of all, of my work fitting into your work and yours into mine and from that intermingling of forces a power being created which will control those forces' (p. 46).

Shared research into the task will replace the giving of orders. She hoped, we may think mistakenly, to see the day when even

19

dismissal from work would be looked upon as a kind of 'doctor's orders'.

However, different situations may need to be co-ordinated one with another. There must therefore be personnel who are skilled at obtaining co-ordinated effort. This is the true function of the manager, and no other kind of control can be justified. 'I have given four principles of organisation. These principles show the basis of control (knowledge) the process of control (recognising the requirements of the situation) and that control is a process. They show us control as self-generated through a process of interweaving of parts. The degree of co-relation is the measure of control; the more complete the reciprocal adjusting the more complete the control.' (M. P. Follett, 1949.)

The theory of leadership has thus moved away from the consideration of dominance patterns. Adult leadership is no longer thought of as a permanent quality which will enable the observer to construct linear dominance structures such as were observable in Murchison's chicks. Leadership is coming to be regarded as a function of the group; overt dominance is thought to be of decreasing significance and usefulness on the higher levels of leadership. Another term, 'group effectiveness' is being used and three of its components held to be: (1) The ability to procure an effective level of functioning, i.e. making use of the available materials to further the purposes of a particular group; (2) the ability to induce group cohesiveness: the power to bind the group and relate members emotionally to each other and to the common task; (3) the ability to maintain stability: the power to resist impairing either (1) or (2) in frustrating conditions (Harris, 1949). One man need not possess all these abilities, or possess any of them all the time. If leadership emerges in response to the situation in which the group finds itself, different persons emerge under different conditions. Harris's slogan is 'every man a leader'.

Similarly the contributors to the Journal of Social Issues (1948) in a symposium on the *Dynamics of the Discussion Group* worked and thought habitually in terms of the distribution of group functions, or roles, among the members, and not in terms of specific leadership behaviour. Thus:

The usual procedure in studies on leadership has been to select

20

certain personality attributes and to attempt to relate them to success or lack of success in known leaders. Implicit in most of this research is the belief that the qualitative components which make for effective leadership are invariant with respect to the situation in which the leadership function is exercised. To the extent that such studies have overlooked the fact that leadership is a complex function of many inter-dependent variables, they have not been fruitful. Leadership behaviour occurs in quite a variety of situations and is determined, in no small measure, by the nature of the particular environment in which the leader perceives himself as functioning as well as by the characteristics of the person who is doing the leading.[1]

Benne and Sheats in the same symposium go on to point out that such a false concept of leadership implies that all 'membership' is really 'followership'. They advocate an analysis of group structure which will consist, firstly, of an analysis of the functions—directed toward problem solution, morale maintenance or the satisfaction of individual needs—performed by the members, and secondly of the nature of the environment which necessitates leadership qualities of a certain type. We shall discuss this again in a later chapter. We may, however, summarise the present discussion and anticipate the later by two short quotations from Parsons, Bales and Shils (1953).

'The stable structure is never, in our data, a "simply organised" one. It is rather one in which differentiated roles have appeared, in which one specialist "undoes" the disturbance to equilibrium created by another, and in turn is dependent upon another to remove the strains which he himself creates" (p. 149).
'As soon as such a (specific and well defined) task is introduced there arises a demand for the performance of the new roles which the task creates' (p. 157).

The fluidity of leadership structure in groups showing the characteristics just described is very valuable. A rigid structure has some disadvantages for the efficiency of the group. A group which is initially unorganised, i.e. has no habitual barriers to communication, may develop a division of labour based on inadequate knowledge of the skills of each member and will therefore be less efficient than it

[1] M. Deutsch, A. Pepitone, A. Zander, *Leadership in the small Group.*

might be. It has been shown in Chapter One that when problems consist of a series of sub-problems, different 'experts' may be required to deal with each step. Each member in the group must have access to every other; otherwise he may be delayed because he has not yet been informed of other parts of the solution, which he must know if he is to make his own contribution. His contribution to the task will be delayed to a degree proportional to the number of intermediaries through which he has to work.

Second, a group may become prematurely structured. By premature, we mean that all members are not as yet in that position in which they may exercise their peculiar skills to greatest effect. Where this happens, a group member who consciously tries to break down the interaction pattern may contribute materially to the efficiency of the group. This is the basic situation in Maier and Solem's (1952) experiment. They constructed groups whose members worked out a simple arithmetical problem, before and after a group discussion. Half the groups contained a trained discussion leader whose general duties were: to encourage the participation of all members, to be permissive and accept the various views expressed, and to encourage the group to think together rather than as individuals. The members of all groups improved the correctness of their estimates after discussion, but groups with a discussion leader improved significantly more. Although this leader himself might be mistaken in his own solution, the fact that he encouraged minorities to state their view increased the number of correct solutions put forward by the members of the group.

Even in a group where roles are distributed in the most functional way, difficulties will arise when a new member joins the group. Instead of the general redistribution of functions which would bear witness to the *interactive* nature of group processes, the new member will tend to be only *added* to the group. He will not be able to show in what capacity he can best serve the group, in which field he is expert, a fact which can only be discovered through free communication and a free choice of activities.

It may be mentioned here that in organisations with a hierarchical structure where some members can only communicate with certain others through intermediaries, often some kind of pre-selection has taken place, that is to say, the organiser of the group has made some kind of assessment concerning the skills of the members and has

22

weighed these up in constructing his hierarchy, because he thought it unlikely that the two members remote from each other in the communication hierarchy would follow each other in the problem-solving sequence. This is how appointments are made in large organisations. That the assumption on which such assessments are made is not always correct is another of Mary Parker Follett's favourite arguments. The man who has worked with the machine may be as expert in his way on possible modifications as the man at the top who approves of the modifications. Often the worker does something about the inconveniences in the officially imposed communications structure by ignoring them.

SUMMARY

(1) 'Leadership', 'power', 'status', 'authority', 'control', 'influence', 'dominance' all involve the ability to elicit a desired response.

(2) A permanent leadership hierarchy can only maintain itself spontaneously where the capacities of the group members are simple and similar.

(3) Differentiation of function occurs when the group task demands several kinds of skills.

(4) Certain skills are acquired as the task is being carried out, thus causing further differentiation.

(5) Restricted communication is characteristic of permanent leadership hierarchies.

(6) Groups will form efficient communication patterns spontaneously if there is a lengthy period of unrestricted communication before the structure becomes permanent.

(7) Leadership is a function of all group members and of the task.

(8) Free communication and a division of labour are not incompatible.

(9) A permanent leadership hierarchy may reduce the problem-solving efficiency of the group,
    (a) because of the delay in information-transmission.
    (b) because of the difficulty in incorporating a new member to greatest advantage.

CHAPTER THREE

Differentiation in the Group: (2) Status Authority

ALL the time we have been concerned with the question: how do people regulate their behaviour with reference to others? Who is affecting whom and in what way? There are many different ways of affecting others; through overt force or through giving information—as in the previous chapter—or because habits of obedience tend to establish themselves—in ways we shall describe in this chapter.

When members can talk freely with other members and affect one another by means of the information they impart and only by those means we have the ideal type of functional authority. When some members cannot communicate to others, or can only communicate certain things—commands, for instance, or certain prescribed categories of information—we have status authority. Restricted communication and permanent status structures are very closely connected. In these circumstances, members differ permanently in the degree to which they possess the ability to elicit a desired response from others and this ability is not necessarily related to skill.

The difference can be briefly summed up by reference to Talcott Parsons' pattern variables. In the previous chapter we described groups in which each member had authority: one could elicit from others the response one desired when others recognised that one knew more about the problem than they did. Such a member's authority is functional. He *achieves* it by virtue of his skill, in *specific* situations where his skill is in demand, and it is *because he is an expert* that he is given this authority. In this chapter we shall describe how it may come about that authority rests on other than functional considerations. In such groups, status is *ascribed* to a man because he is that *particular* man and no other, because he is Joe himself. Joe will be able to use his authority *diffusely*, in many different

24

situations; it is not specific to certain problems. In such groups, the same members tend to be always in authority.

In examining the divorce of leadership from skill we have to show in each case (a) how the communication structure becomes a permanent structure, and (b) how status considerations become attached to it.

ASSUMPTION ONE

Let a routine be established in the group.

In the previous chapter we pursued the process of differentiation in the group until we arrived at the point where each man is free to perform the functions for which he is most fitted. We supposed that the task was such that a variety of skills was needed at different stages of problem solving and that therefore every man was a leader at some time or another. Suppose now that in the history of the group the same problem has frequently arisen. In that case the sequence in which contributions to the task are made will tend to become habitual. It will become habitual for certain members to speak before others do, for Jack to wait until Joe has spoken. In this way, restrictions in free communication are brought about. The need for orderliness and predictability of behaviour will further accentuate this tendency toward restricted communication. Once such a routine has become established, it tends to remain whether the task is a routine one or not. Thus the communication structure may become independent of the problem to be solved. Parsons, Bales and Shils describe how this affects the status of members:

'In so far as a given person "gets on the right track" and receives positive reactions from other members, he will be reinforced in his direction of movement, and will tend to keep on talking. He will "generalise" from the premises, logical and emotional, which underlay his original successful attempt. . . . And reciprocally, the other members will "generalise" from his earlier attempts, gratifying in some sense to them, to an expectation of further effective behaviour on his part. The member begins to build a "specialised role". In so far as the activity he performs is felt to be important in terms of the functional problems of the group, its goals and value norms, the "status" of the member will begin to rise. There will be a "generalisation" from the specific *performance* of the person to a

25

qualitatively ascribed "position" in the group which bears a rank relation to other positions similarly developed' (p. 133).

Such settled expectations as to different members' 'rights' to communicate is one of the elements which define a stable status structure. It then becomes legitimate to speak of status as a permanent attribute and one not necessarily connected with skill in solving a particular aspect of a problem. Once a man's status becomes generalised, his ability to elicit the response he desires is less closely bound up with technical skill. At the same time, his position in the communication structure has become fixed.

ASSUMPTION TWO

Let us assume likes and dislikes in the group.

Another manner in which a member's position may become fixed derives from the fact that a man may like one member of the group better than another. The problem presented by such sentiments is discussed at length in Chapter Seven. At present we must content ourselves with assuming the existence of these sentiments without inquiring into their origin.

Newcomb (1947–8) points out that if one dislikes a person or is offended by him, one may not speak to him again and thus one shuts oneself off from communications which might modify the previous attitude of either party to the dispute. Such restricted communication may be overt, in a refusal to meet, or where this is impossible, covert, by taking as little notice of the communication as possible. It is therefore not unreasonable to suppose that there is a sense in which members do not hear what is being said by those they do not care for. These mechanisms, called by Newcomb 'autistic mechanisms', may operate quite generally against low status members. Indeed, defining status as the ability to elicit a desired response, a man who is not listened to by others is by definition a man of low status.

It is important to remember that in a long continuing group it is not necessary to assume that all members are present when a communication is made by one member to another. It is much more likely that there will be members who see much of one another and less of other members of the group. If such a group persists over a considerable time, communication will travel through the links

26

created by personal friendships. A sociogram[1] of such a group based on liking may therefore be transformed into a structure showing where communication is easy and where difficult. That this is so is abundantly clear from the literature on rumours. Thus Festinger, Cartwright, *et al.* (1948) report that rumours in a neighbourhood group where communication paths are not formally determined, are transmitted from friend to friend.[2] Similarly, it is generally acknowledged that in large organisations the members will tend to disregard the formal structure imposed upon them and communicate through 'informal', i.e. friendship channels.

Even when members who like one another cannot physically exclude those they like less well, they will speak to them less frequently.

The presence of autistic mechanisms has a further affect. It makes the most popular, rather than the most skilled, man the leader. He who has the greatest number of friendships, in a group where members can communicate to one another in the absence of other members, is at the centre of the network through which communication is transmitted. A popular man has therefore easy and direct access to information, an important function in the group and one that confers status (Bales, 1951). In these circumstances the popular person becomes powerful because he can choose to transmit information to some and withhold it from others. In this way, he is enabled to gain status in two other ways enumerated by Bales: indirect access to resources (because he is able to make other members more, or less, productive according to the amount of information that he transmits to and from them) and control, the ability to gain approval for his proposals (because there may be nothing to compel him to present all the facts of a situation to each member, and also because they like him). A man is almost always able to elicit the response he desires from his friends.

The fact that a popular member of a group stands at the node of the communication paths means also that he can gauge opinion in the group better than other members. He will have more insight into the feelings of group members. A man who is skilled in social relations and therefore able to gain the liking of other members easily, is

---

[1] For a discussion of sociometric techniques see chapter on the evolution of likes and dislikes and Appendix.
[2] E.g. Back, Festinger, *et al.* (1950). Festinger, Schachter and Bach (1950).

27

likely to gain status because of the position in the communication network that his popularity will bring him.[1]

In all these ways, the ties of friendship may resemble channels of communication quite closely, at the same time defining the status structure of the group.

ASSUMPTION THREE

Let members differ in the amount they wish to speak.

So far we have assumed that all members would speak roughly the same amount were it not for differences in skill or popularity. Plainly the contributions made by members to the conversation will depend to some extent on the task to be performed and on the presence of those members to whom they like to talk. All the same, there is evidence that when these influences are disregarded for the purposes of analysis 'each person has constant and invariant relationships in the frequency of his actions and inactions (i.e. silences) no matter with whom he interacts'. This hypothesis was tested by Goldman-Eisler (1951) using a number of students each of whom was paired with every other and allowed a half-hour discussion. By noting the length and frequency of speech and silence, she was able to prove the validity of her hypothesis. Borghatta and Bales (1953) took the point a little further. They measured the communication rates of members of groups, and then regrouped the members in such a way that there were groups of 'high contributors', (i.e. frequent or lengthy speakers), groups of 'low contributors', and groups in which there was one high, one medium and one low contributor. They found that in these circumstances, the low contributors spoke a little more frequently than before, since they were given a better chance in a group in which no one dominated verbally, but still not as much as the high contributors. The high contributors spoke less frequently than before, presumably simply because there is a limit to the amount that can be said in any given period of time. Groups in which there was one of each kind has the most *interaction*, since everyone was able to speak at his preferred level. This implies, first, that Goldman-Eisler is right in her hypothesis that each person has a characteristic level of communication congenial to himself, and, second, that this level is to some extent affected by the characteristic levels of communication of other members of the group. Borghatta

[1] See pages 135–7.

28

and Bales express the relationship in the following formula: The contributions made by any member are a function of the ratio

$$\frac{\text{own characteristic rate of communication}}{\text{average characteristic communication rates of other members}}$$

There are thus 'natural' restrictions on communication, attributable to the personalities of the members.

The fact that some people talk more than others has some important effects. For although any remark made in the group is, of course, heard by all present, it is often directed at a particular member. The recipient of such a communication tends in turn to direct his answer to his interlocutor. Moreover, voluble members produce a greater stimulus to the group than quiet members: people will answer them back, to agree, disagree or elaborate. This means that frequent speakers are also likely to be frequently addressed. Accordingly, Bales (1951) finds that not only *communication rates* but also *interaction rates* are characteristic for members of groups engaged in a task. The most frequent initiator of interaction is also the most frequent recipient. Moreover, the most frequent speaker speaks most to the one next to him in communication rank and so on down the scale. Everyone tends to address voluble members, quiet as well as frequent speakers, but since quiet members are quiet, frequent speakers converse mostly with one another.

Frequent speakers are more likely to interact with one another than with quiet members. This means, of course, that sub-groupings are likely to evolve within the group, based on this exclusiveness of interaction. Such groupings are of necessity more frequently pairs than trios, and more frequently trios than foursomes. Sometimes relationships of the type A–B, B–C, but not A–C, occur.[1]

All this would be irrelevant to a discussion of status were it not for the fact, later to be discussed at length, that in many circumstances interaction between members tends to make them like one another and that this liking grows as interaction increases.[2] Voluble members should accordingly like one another better than quiet members. If we examine the content of the communications made by frequent and infrequent speakers, we find that this is so. Mills (1953), for instance, ran a number of three-person discussion-groups for half-hourly discussions. In these groups there tend to be two highly active mem-

[1] See Appendix for further discussion.　　　　[2] See page 91.

29

bers and one less active one. We find that the two active members tend to support one another more than they support the third member of the group. In this way the active members reinforce for one another the influence that they possess. Whether this is due to the fact that influential members are allowed to speak more frequently than others or whether voluble members subsequently gain power is an interesting speculation. In any case, differences in communication rates are accompanied by differences in the interaction of members, and these in turn are connected with differences in the content of communications. The support that highly active members lend to one another reinforces their high status and maintains the low status of less active members.

Voluble members maintain high status not only because they support each other. Some other facts need to be stated in this connection. Because voluble members are more frequently addressed than others, they are likely to be better informed. Also, since the group can act only on the information at its disposal (whether information about a task or about the feelings of members), voluble members are bound to affect the group more than quiet ones purely by the fact that they are quick to impart such information. Moreover, there seems to be in the minds of many people what one might be inclined to call a confusion between volubility and productivity. Bates, in an unpublished study quoted by Riecken and Homans (1954), shows that the rank order of members in number of interactions received correlated highly with their rank order in a test in which each member was asked to rank the others in terms of their contribution to carrying out the assigned task of the group. In a quite different context, Norfleet (1948) reports that in discussion groups analysed by her, members who spoke a good deal were rated by the group as 'more productive' than the quieter members. Indeed the correlation of productivity rating and degree of participation was of the order of 0·95. She warns, however, that 'mere quantity of contribution will probably not correlate so highly in groups where members have not learned to limit their contributions to those which are productive'. Nevertheless, it is very possible that a confusion exists in the minds of the members, which is likely to keep this correlation high in many circumstances.[1]

[1] Readers may wonder whether volubility, productivity or popularity is a greater asset in status gaining. It may therefore be relevant to add that Norfleet finds that the members regarded as productive are addressed more frequently than those who are

ASSUMPTION FOUR

Let differences in status be recognised by members of the group.
It is perhaps not very fruitful to argue whether consciousness of
low status determines the low rate of activity or whether the low rate
of activity depresses other members' expectations of the value of what
the low contributors have to say. The evidence presented in this
chapter leaves no doubt, however, that the two go together. In
groups where many members may have possible contributions to
make, low status members are likely to defer in their views to high
status (or/and voluble) speakers. We have seen from Norfleet that
voluble members are likely to be regarded as productive. To this we
now add a finding from Hurwitz, *et al.* (in Cartwright and Zander,
1953) that at a conference of social workers there were members who
felt that their contributions were not important enough to be voiced,
an experience which most of us will have had at one time or another.
If a man does not speak, his views are not likely to be taken into
account. A quiet man has less control over the group. We have seen
how frequent speakers support one another rather than the quiet
member. The quiet member recognises his position and behaves
accordingly. Thus Bales (1951) finds that voluble members show
more 'attempted answers' on his observation chart.[1] (See also foot-
note to previous page.) This means that they give their opinions and
make suggestions as to what is to be done more frequently than quiet
members, who tend mostly to show their reactions to what has been

very popular. Bales (in Parsons, Bales and Shils, 1953) shows also that frequent
speakers are more frequently rated as 'having the best ideas' and 'doing the most to
guide discussion' than rated highly as liked. In many groups one may have to choose
between these two types of behaviour. The crux of the matter cannot be discussed till
later. See p. 103 in the chapter on the emergence of likes and dislikes.

[1] If there were unlimited time available for the discussion and solution of problems,
the fact that members' communication rates differ would not matter. If, however, there
is a time limit—and the greater the urgency of the problem the less time will be devoted
to discussion before a suggested solution is acted upon—members may feel dissatisfied
because they have been unable to speak to the extent preferred by them, and they may
feel disgruntled about the proposed course of action. Plainly the larger the group, the
less opportunity there will be for each member to speak as much as he wants to in a
limited period of time. In a small group each member has more opportunity to speak;
in a larger group each member has less time in any given period to make his own
(possibly valuable) contribution. Hare (1952) reports that groups of boys felt there had
been ample time for discussion in five-member groups, but not in groups of twelve
members each, and these latter groups also felt dissatisfied with the conclusions they
had reached. The quieter members are pushed into the background because of the
shortage of time, the voluble members exercise a restraining influence upon the group
and the structure will become stabilised with the voluble members 'at the centre of
thing'. The material presented under the next assumption will make this clearer.

suggested and therefore score highly in such areas as agreement and disagreement, praise and blame. Similarly, Strodtbeck (1951) finds that in the family voluble speakers tend to get their own way more frequently than other members when there is disagreement. There seems to be some point in nagging after all!

One reason for the low status of quiet members is probably to be found in the fact, to be discussed in detail in Chapter Nine, that a period of information–exchange precedes the period of decision-taking. Except in situations where proposed actions are voted upon, one cannot usually carry a meeting merely by expressing disagreement.[1] The group requires at least a show of reason before it commits itself to a course of action and this necessitates participation at the stage of information–exchange.

A quiet member may lose a lot by not weighing in at this stage. Unfortunately even when he does speak, a low status member cannot always gain the ear of the group; he suffers because of the autistic mechanisms previously described. A high-status member is required to give far less justification for his proposals than other members. He has the advantages of being considered an authority, a confusion of thought resting upon a pun.

Thus once status differences are recognised by the members of the group, we find that the skill which earlier we postulated as conferring status is often itself a socially determined characteristic. Consciousness of high status improves a man's performance and increases the tendency of other members to see his performance as good. This is shown, for instance, by Harvey (1953). He instructed members of groups in which there was a sharp awareness of status differences to play a game rather like darts and to estimate their own (and other people's) performance. He found that members whose status in the group was high, tended to over-estimate their future performance, and in this distortion of judgement they were supported by the other members of the group. A member of low status tended less to over-

---

[1] Even when proposed courses of action are voted upon, low-status members may be at a disadvantage. Suppose that a group is organised in a hierarchical way, each sub-group, in order of status, voting on the issue and handing down the result to the next level. This is equivalent to saying that decisions in a sub-network are made by majority rule. The information transmitted to the group at the next level of centrality may now cause conflict of data at this level. But the weight of the top level is behind it and therefore it is transmitted even further down the line. In this way a small resolute group in a stratified network may have considerable influence on the action—as governed by information—of a number of members considerably larger than the number that composed the original sub-network (Penrose, 1952).

estimation and might in fact under-estimate himself, and the group shared his poor opinion of himself.

Sometimes members of the group take an active part to see that high-status members perform well. Thus Whyte (1943) reports that in the street-corner gang, the performance of low-status members who were able to do well when bowling with other teams deteriorated markedly when matching skills with high-status members of the gang. He attributes this to the fact that other members consistently heckled and jeered during the contests. High-status members get positive support from the group and low-status members are given negative support when exercising their skills.[1] The structure of the group is in this way stabilised. Whyte also points out that low-status members may make good suggestions, but that they are not taken up by the members unless the leader accepts and repeats them.

Where consciousness of status exists, communication may be restricted in another way, in that only certain types of communication are transmitted. Thus Kelley (1951) formed groups of college students and told them they would be divided into two groups. One group would send messages to the other group, instructing them how to place bricks in a certain pattern. Any member could send written messages to any other member. When the groups were separated he told one group that placing the bricks was the more important and skilled task, and the other group that sending the messages was the more important. In fact all groups did the same work—placing bricks—and the instructions which purported to come from the other group were standard messages sent by the experimenter. The group which had been told that laying bricks was the better task and who therefore thought of themselves as doing important work, were called by Kelley 'high status'. The group which had been told that sending messages was the better work, and who therefore were not doing the work that was considered the more important, Kelley called 'low status'. Finally there were also control groups, who were given no indication of their status.

The experimenter collected the notes written by the subjects, who

---

[1] This interesting phenomenon may tentatively be explained in the following way. It is an error to regard the leader as excelling in one function only. The group wishes to maintain an integrated ideology and the leader emerges because of the *configuration* of qualities he possesses. Those who were good at bowling, the manifest determinant of status in this group, but did not live up to the total group ideology, were by this means kept down.

were led to think that these would be transmitted to the other group. Kelley found that high-status members tended to criticise the low level, and that the low status members criticised one another. Low-status members also frequently expressed their difficulty at understanding the task, although in fact they did not make significantly more errors than the high-status groups. The high-status members were very careful not to send criticisms of their own job or their confusion in it to low-status members. The lows, on the other hand, did not criticise the high-status members. The general effect was, of course, to confirm the status differences of which the group was aware. (In the control group the number of critical messages was greater, but they were sent impartially within and between the two sub-groups.)

Low-status members sought to escape from a situation which they felt to be unpleasant by sending large numbers of messages irrelevant to the performance of the task, both within their own group and to the other group. The amount of irrelevant matter communicated will obviously have an effect on the quality of the performance as well as on the morale of the groups.

We shall return to Kelley's experiment in a later chapter, for we have not exhausted all that may be said of the effect of consciousness of status differences. But we cannot carry our argument further until we have discussed at length the function of sentiments, in particular of norms and friendships, in the group.[1]

ASSUMPTION FIVE

Let members interact within a competitive situation.

Deutsch (1949) contrasts co-operative and competitive groups in the following way:

'In a *co-operative social situation* the goals for the individuals or sub-units in the situation under consideration have the following characteristics: the goal regions for each of the individuals or sub-units in the situation are defined so that a goal-region can be entered (to some degree) by any given individual or sub-unit only if all the individuals or sub-units under consideration can also enter their respective goal regions (to some degree). In a *competitive social situation* . . . if a goal region is entered by any individual or sub-unit . . . the other individuals or sub-units will, to

---

[1] The discussion is carried further on pages 102–3.

34

some degree, be unable to reach their respective goals in the social situation under consideration.'

In his analysis of co-operative and competitive groups in action Deutsch shows some interesting differences between them. For instance, competing members are careful to withhold information from one another, with the result that members of the co-operative group learn from one another to a much greater extent than do competing members. Members in competition also communicate less frequently with one another and are less friendly.

A group whose members are in competition with one another is like a badly organised or muddled group. In the one case the members deliberately hinder one another, in the other they are in each other's way by accident.[1]

Mintz (1951) put subjects in a position where all could attain their ends provided they organised themselves. The subjects were required to pull a wedge attached to a line and rod out of a narrow-necked bottle.

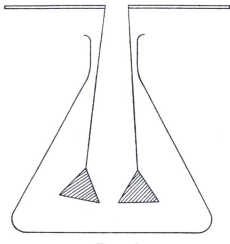

Figure 1

If two subjects tried to do so at the same time, their wedges would jam and their attempts would fail. Normally, however, subjects

[1] For a further discussion of the need for organisation see Chapter 5.

managed to deal adequately with the problem. But when Mintz introduced stress into the situation by allowing water to enter the bottle from below and giving money to those who extracted their wedge before it got wet, the subjects did not take time to organise themselves efficiently and they frequently got into such a muddle that all their wedges were jammed in the bottle.

A co-operative group evolves a division of labour. Each member will prefer to perform that part of the task in which he feels himself to be expert. He is recognised as able in his sphere by other members and thus a voluntary division of labour comes about. In this situation if one man nears his goal so do all the others in the group. A good division of labour implies that members work according to a commonly recognised plan. Before A can choose his plan of work, he must know what B is planning to do. Both can only work at their best if communication is perfect. In a competitive situation on the other hand it is important to conceal one's strategy from other members (Simon 1947, also Follett op. cit.). In this way communication becomes restricted.

SUMMARY

A stable status structure is one in which members possess permanently to different degrees the ability to elicit a desired response.

(1) When a group has solved a series of similar problems, members whose skill has been used for the solution of these problems tend to acquire authority in situations where their skill is not necessarily required. In this way communication becomes restricted and authority becomes divorced from skill.

(2) (a) Members who like one another will tend to respond to one another more frequently than to those they like less well. In this way communication becomes restricted and authority becomes divorced from skill.

(b) If some members of the group are able to communicate in the absence of other members, a popular member will be at the centre of the communication network. He will have more access to information than other members. In this way communication will be restricted. Access to information confers status.

(c) If members of the group are able to communicate in the

36

absence of other members, a popular member can give or withhold information. In this way he will be able to control the decisions of other members.

(d) By virtue of his position in the network a popular member has: (i) greater direct and indirect access to resources.
(ii) more control over other members.
(iii) more insight into the behaviour of other members.
(iv) more opportunity to gauge opinion in the group.

(e) If some members are able to communicate in the absence of other members, a sociogram based on liking may be regarded as a structure showing the relative ease of communication between various members.

(f) The contributions made by unpopular members tend to be disregarded. In this way communication will become restricted and authority divorced from skill.

(3) (a) There are natural restrictions on communication attributable to the personalities of members of the groups. The contributions made by any member are a function of the ratio:

$$\frac{\text{own characteristic rate of communication}}{\text{average characteristic communication rates of other members}}$$

(b) Frequent speakers are frequently addressed.

(c) Frequent speakers speak to one another and tend to support one another. In this way they reinforce each other's high status and maintain the lower status of other members.

(d) Voluble members are likely to be regarded as productive.

(e) If some members can communicate with one another in the absence of other members, those who meet frequently are better informed about group affairs. Access to information confers status.

(4) In a given period of time members of a small group can contribute more to a discussion than members of a larger group. Quieter members are thus given more of a chance in the small group than in the larger one. In the latter situation they may feel that their opinions have not been given sufficient consideration and they may become disgruntled and dissatisfied with the solution.

(5) (a) When status differences are recognised by members of the group, low status members tend to inhibit their own communications. Thus communication becomes restricted and authority divorced from skill.

(b) Frequent speakers make more suggestions and give their opinions relatively more frequently than quiet members. Quiet members tend to communicate relatively more frequently their approval or disapproval of what has been suggested by the frequent speakers.

(c) Consciousness of high status improves performance and increases the tendency of other members to perceive a performance as good. The opposite is true in the case of low-status members. Skill itself is therefore to some extent a socially determined characteristic.

(d) Consciousness of status differences may affect the content of communication in the following way:

(i) high-status members criticise low-status members;
(ii) high-status members do not criticise one another;
(iii) low-status members express more confusion with the task although they make no more errors;
(iv) low-status members feel they cannot make such good suggestions as high-status members;

(e) Contributions made by unpopular members are ignored.

(6) If time is limited or the group is large the number of contributions made by less voluble members will decrease.

(7) High-status members get more positive and low-status members get more negative support when exercising their skills.

(8) The more unpleasant one's position in a status hierarchy the greater the amount of irrelevant communication. According to this criterion the following is the order of pleasantness of position in the group:

(a) secure high status,

(b) mobile low status,

(c) insecure high and immobile low status.

(9) In groups where decisions are transmitted by majority vote, a

small resolute group may control a large number of indifferent members.

(10) A badly organised or unorganised group, or a group with status conflict, resembles a competitive group:

the attainment of aims by one member hinders other members in the performance of their own work;

members withhold information from one another;

members communicate hostile feeling and criticisms;

members communicate a great deal of material unrelated to the task.

CHAPTER FOUR

The Spread of Information[1]

MANY variables need to be considered when describing the
processes of group life. Since it is impossible to consider
them all simultaneously, one way of introducing some order
into description of this kind is to start with the very simplest assumptions about the group and to complicate them gradually by bringing
in new variables. Then one can consider the effect that such new
variables have on the relationships already stated. In the earlier
chapters of this book the assumptions have been so simple and often
so general that one will not find outside the laboratory groups
governed solely by the mechanisms described. In the present chapter
we are even more extreme. The group members are assumed to be no
more than automata and all members are assumed to be completely
similar. The members' functions are restricted to transmitting without alteration all the information at their disposal. They may not
withhold it, forget it, misunderstand it or do any of the things which,
often to our irritation, real people do. The members differ initially
only in the kind of information they possess; no member's information is more important than that of any other member. The spread of
information in this hypothetical situation is therefore determined
solely and fundamentally by the communication structure of the
groups. Because we shall assume that there are no distinguishing
marks that differentiate one person from another, we shall, in tracing
the spread of information through the group, do no more than make

[1] Readers who wish to pursue the type of analysis outlined in this Chapter are
referred to the mathematical literature on topology and network theory, of which a
good bibliography may be found in Christie, L. S., Luce, R. D., and Macy, J. (*Communication and Learning in Task orientated Groups* (1952). The main body of their book
is simpler and has a more obvious sociological relevance than the literature their bibliography refers to; even so, it is very difficult in places. The simplest approach to the subject may be found in Bavelas, A. (1948)—'A Mathematical Model of Group Structures', *Applied Anthropology*. An interesting discussion of very similar problems is
to be found in Lewin, K., *Field Theory in Social Science*, Chapters V, X and Appendix.

explicit some of the mathematical properties that communication networks possess. It is the bare bones of group structure that will become apparent, before they are clothed with the elaborations of group life. Such severity has an elegance of its own.

Its use for us will be that it enables us to describe differences between groups structured in various ways. We showed in the previous chapter how restrictions in communication may come about. These restrictions form all kinds of patterns of communication.[1] In this chapter we do not concern ourselves with the origin of these restrictions; we shall take it for granted that they exist and set about describing them. Once such restrictions do exist they will affect the transmission of information in the group. This will itself have consequences for other activities in the group, such as learning and organisation, which will be discussed in the next chapter, but the main importance of the concepts now to be described is that they provide us with a method in terms of which we can distinguish between groups which differ in the manner and extent to which they have restricted their communication. Before we tackle any further problems we must fix firmly in our minds the concepts in terms of which structure can be analysed and the effects which can be attributed to structure when it alone is regarded as the determinant of group characteristics.

The basic elements of the description of group structure are the group members and the communication channels or 'links' between them. These channels determine the network and the structure of the group. Strictly speaking, a *network* is defined as a set of links between members who use all communication channels available to them; a *structure* is a network in which some channels are, for reasons not further examined in this chapter, neglected.

ASSUMPTION ONE

Let all members be exactly alike.

This assumption is valid throughout the chapter. On its basis it will be possible to attribute all differences in the behaviour of mem-

---

[1] If the method now to be outlined is to be used for practical purposes, for describing the structure of a group, care has to be taken in specifying what types of relationships will define the structure. In concrete description we have to specify, for instance, whether we call a man central because he is well-informed (centrality in the information structure), well-liked (centrality in the sentiment structure), of high status (centrality in the power structure), and so on.

41

bers to their position in the network and to nothing else. All members will be subject to the same external constraints. If, therefore, we find differentiation—differences in the behaviour of members which allow us to distinguish between one member and another—it is bound to have arisen in the course of information-transmission, and it is bound to be due to network characteristics and to nothing else.

ASSUMPTION TWO

Let all members communicate through all the links at their disposal.

Unless the contrary is explicitly stated, it is assumed in this chapter that a communication channel is never ignored. When a member has a piece of information, it is assumed that he will transmit it to all the members with whom he is connected. These members in turn are assumed to communicate the information they have received through all the channels at their disposal. In this way information spreads through the network. We also assume for the moment that no time has to be spent in the hearing, reading, writing, or understanding of the messages. In the next chapter we shall relax this assumption.

ASSUMPTION THREE

Let the number of members be varied in a group in which each member is directly linked with every other member.

The size of networks may be defined either by the number of members included, or by a more composite definition in which the number and position of the links is taken into account as well. If there are links between all members in a group of n members, there will be $\frac{1}{2}n(n-1)$ links.[1] In considering the effect of an increase in the number of members in a group in which all members may speak freely, the number of channels of communication it would be necessary to maintain can be calculated through the same formula. One factor which makes for a great complexity of relationships in groups is the fact that the number of links increases very rapidly with an

[1] This formula is arrived at in the following way. Each member has a link to every other member through which he communicates, but he does not communicate with himself. In a group of n members, therefore, each member will have $(n-1)$ links. This is multiplied by n, the number of members in the group, if we want the total number of links, for the whole group, which is therefore $n(n-1)$. But in doing this we are guilty of double-counting; we have counted the link AB (and all other links) twice, once as from A to B, and once as from B to A. Therefore we divide through by 2 and arrive at the formula $\frac{1}{2}n(n-1)$.

increase in the number of members (Kephart, 1949, 1950). The addition of one member requires as many new links as there were members before the new recruit joined.

For a three-member group the number of links would be three.

„	four-	„	„	„	„	six.
„	five-	„	„	„	„	ten.
„	six-	„	„	„	„	fifteen.

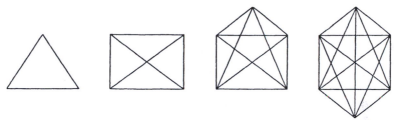

Figure 1

By the same token, the number of structures which may evolve out of the networks would increase sharply as the number of members increases if Assumption Two were abolished, i.e., if members were allowed to choose with whom they would communicate. We shall consider this possibility in Chapter Five.

ASSUMPTION FOUR

Let the number of members be held constant and the number of links varied.

It does not always happen that each member can communicate directly with every other member. Other considerations closely bound up with an intuitive meaning of size enter when groups with the same membership-totals differ in the number of links between the members. The proportion of links to members is, however, too imprecise a measure to be useful, for we shall see that much depends on the position of the links.

In the three five-member networks illustrated in Figure 2, we find four, five and ten links respectively. Suppose that all members can receive and send messages simultaneously and that each transmission from member to member takes one minute. How long will it take before all members are in possession of the same information, each starting out with a different bit? In the totally connected network the time will be one minute, since only one link separates any two members. In the circle the time will be two minutes, since for each member there are two others who can be reached directly and two to whom the neighbours have to transmit in the second minute the

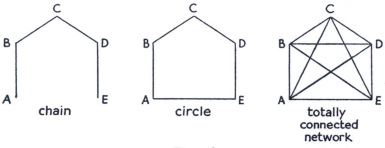

chain   circle   totally
connected
network

Figure 2

information they have just received. In the chain there are two members who must communicate through four links (i.e. through three other members) and though some members will possess complete information before then, four minutes have to elapse before every member of the group is completely informed.

We may therefore say that the greater the number of links between members, the sooner all members will be equally informed, provided all members communicate through all the links at their disposal. It is also clear that the more links there are in the network, the greater is the number of members who will gain information after only one transmission.

ASSUMPTION FIVE

Let the number of links and the number of members be the same in two groups.

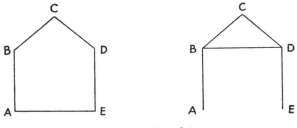

Figures 3 and 4

44

Counting the number of links is not a perfect way of describing a network. Consider the two networks illustrated in Figures 3 and 4. Both have the same number of links (five) but information will spread more rapidly through Figure 3 than through Figure 4, because in the latter there is one communication, that between A and E, which has to be made in three steps, whereas in Figure 3 these two are directly linked. We must, therefore, have recourse to a more refined index. This is to be found by totalling the number of links, direct and indirect, which exist between any two members of the group. This is done as follows:

For Figure 3		For Figure 4	
Members	*Links needed*	*Members*	*Links needed*
A to B	1	A to B	1
A to C	2	A to C	2
A to D	2	A to D	2
A to E	1	A to E	3
Total	6	Total	8

The total number of links connecting A in Figure 3 to every other member is therefore six, and for A in Figure 4 it is eight. Since A in Figure 3 is in exactly the same position as any other member, the total sum of distances between all members in Figure 3 is $5 \times 6 = 30$. In Figure 4 only E is in the same position as A; B and D are also in a similar position, the total for either of them being $1 + 1 + 1 + 2 = 5$. The total for member C is $1 + 2 + 1 + 2 = 6$. The total sum of distances between all members in Figure 4 is therefore

$$(2 \times 8) + (2 \times 5) + 6 = 32.$$

This sum is obviously important if one wishes to know how much information will be held in common by members of a group after a certain lapse of time. With certain exceptions, the greater the total sum of distances between all members, the fewer people will have received information in a given period of time.

A further measure, and the best if we wish to know the minimum period of time required for everyone in a network to be informed, is the *diameter*. The diameter is the shortest distance between the two members furthest apart in a network. In the totally connected network shown in Figure 2, every member is directly connected by one link with every other member. All members are equally 'far apart';

the shortest distance between them is one link; therefore d = 1. In the circle, any member can reach any other in at least two steps, therefore d = 2. (It is, of course, possible to get from A to D through B and C, but that is not the *shortest* distance between them and it is therefore ruled out.) In the chain A and E are furthest apart; the one has to reach the other in no less than four steps, therefore d = 4.

To be quite precise, therefore, it will be best to rewrite our previous generalisation in the following way, splitting it into two separate propositions. The smaller the sum of all distances between members, the more members will be better informed after one transmission. The smaller the diameter the sooner all members will be informed completely.

There is another reason why this is a better formulation, for there may be what could be called 'superfluous links' in a network. If, for instance, the diameter of a network is three, it may be irrelevant that a number of members can communicate in less than three steps. In Figure 5, for instance, there are a number of links, such as, for instance, links AD and BE, which do nothing to reduce the diameter although they reduce the sum of distances between members. Superfluous links may, however, be very important, especially when there is a danger that there are disturbances in communication. This case is discussed later in this and in the next chapter.[1]

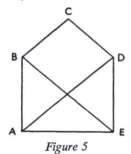

Figure 5

It has been shown that when the sum of all distances from one member to every other member is calculated, this sum is found to differ for different members. For rough and ready work it is simplest to distinguish between members by counting the number of links at the disposal of every member. For precision a more complex measure is used. We find the distances between one member and all the other members of the group in the way shown on the previous page under Assumption Five, that is, by counting the number of links needed to connect that member to others in the group. The number arrived at in this way is then compared with the total number of distances between all members and all others. In this way we arrive at the con-

[1] Other types of superfluous linkage will of course occur if one member has no information or if two members always possess the same information.

cept of *centrality*.[1] It measures the *centrality* of each member. The centrality index of any member $X =$

$$\frac{\text{sum of distances from every member to every other member}}{\text{sum of distances from member } X \text{ to every other member}}$$

ASSUMPTION SIX

Let the centrality indices of members differ.

The concept of a centrality index is a very fruitful one for the description of the characteristics of networks. The consequences of differences in centrality will be referred to again and again in subsequent chapters. In Figure 6, the centrality indices of members in various types of network are illustrated.

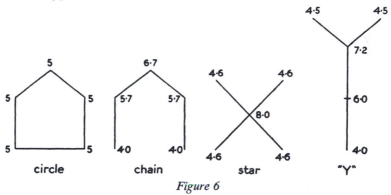

Figure 6

There are several points of interest to be noted in the networks shown in Figure 6. Firstly, the networks differ in the number of levels of centrality discernible in them. This must have important consequences in all groups where hierarchical differences are described. In the circle all members are on the same level; none is more central than any other. In the star there are two levels and the differences in centrality are very marked indeed. In the chain there are three, and in the Y four levels. Secondly, the central member really deserves his name. He is closer to the other members than anyone else. If the other members wish to reach each other by the shortest possible route, they are compelled to communicate through

---

[1] The numerator is a constant for any group. If, therefore, we are interested only in one network, we may substitute any convenient number for it. But if we wish to compare centrality patterns in a number of networks the numerator must be stated in full, for it differs for different networks.

him. We have already seen that in the course of the communication process some members will be in possession of all available information while others are still waiting to have it transmitted to them. The more central a member, the sooner he will be in possession of all the information at the disposal of the group. And the greater the number of levels the greater his advantage over other members.

The greater the number of levels the greater his advantage over others, for the longer it will take before the information at his disposal will reach the peripheral members. If therefore a decision has to be made in a hurry he may very well be tempted to make it without consulting those members who are still waiting to have the rest of the information transmitted to them. Thirdly, further differentiation may occur in a group after a number of transmissions due to differences in the centrality levels of the members. At the end of only one transmission, central members will be better informed than others because of their position in the network. The fact that in the middle phase of the communication process the central members are better informed than others has another important consequence. We have shown that influence is closely related to the possession of information. There are therefore times when the central person or sub-group will not only possess more information but be able to exert more influence. Fourthly, if the central man is fed most of the information, he is most likely to spot any discrepancies between items as they come to him. Generally speaking, therefore, the central members are also in the best position for correcting errors. Conversely, if the central members make a mistake, the chances that it will be corrected are relatively small.

Finally, the central member is the most indispensable because if he does not transmit information, the diameter of the group increases more markedly than would be the case with any other member. To sum up, because of the functions which the central member performs by virtue of his position, such members are very valuable and the loss of such members is likely to have more serious consequences for the group than the loss of a peripheral member would have had.

ASSUMPTION SEVEN

Let there be disturbances in the communication channels.

The question of indispensability is an interesting one. Not only are some members more indispensable than others, but some networks will suffer more than others from the destruction of a member or a link. Consider the circle: if any member or any link be missing, the network becomes a chain; and communication, though slower, will still be possible between the remaining members. But if a member or a link be missing from a chain, some members of the group might find themselves isolated. The group would be smaller than before, or it might now consist of two networks isolated from one another. This possibility may be indicated by a number k. Where $k = 1$, the destruction of one link will isolate one or more members, as in the chain; where $k = 2$, two links must be destroyed before this can happen, as in the circle. For a totally connected group with n members, $k = n - 1$.

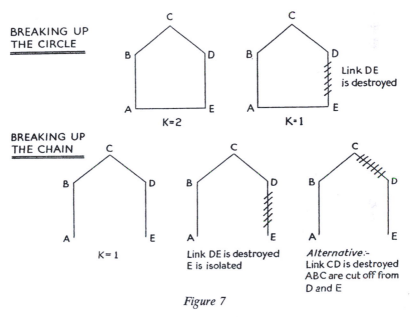

Figure 7

A break in a link between members is of course less interesting for the study of small groups than other kinds of interference, such as misunderstandings, the inhibition of communication through differences in the status of two communicating members, and other types of restricted communication such as were discussed in the previous chapter. Whatever the origin of a disturbance, however, it is important to remember that groups with different networks will differ in the ease with which members can be isolated from their fellow members. The ease with which a member may be cut off from the group can thus be seen as one of the elements making for differentiation between members. In Figure 8, for instance, the disappearance of link CD would isolate members DEF but the disappearance of link EF would hardly impair the working of the group. Similarly in Figure 9, the disappearance of member C is a more serious matter than the disappearance of any other member. It will be noted that he is also more central.

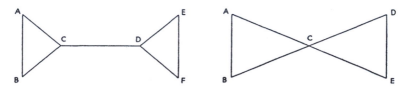

Figures 8 and 9

Obviously, where only one member or link connects two clusters of members, the possibility of disruption is more immediate. In such cases, moreover, if the crucial member or link fails to transmit accurately there is no way of correcting the error. A concrete example of such cases may be found where one man is a member of two groups, for instance when a committee appoints one of its members to act as its representative on another committee. In this way it becomes possible to think of a member as the connection between two groups. This will be useful when we wish to analyse sub-networks and the degree to which sub-networks are dependent on one another.

ASSUMPTION EIGHT

Let some members be more closely connected with the network than others.

Obviously, there may be members who have so many links to others that they are unlikely to be ever completely cut off from all other members. Others may be in a more vulnerable position. In many larger groups there may be clusters of members closely con-

50

nected with one another, but with few links to other clusters. Figures 8 and 9 give an example. One can identify sub-networks in any group where the number of links between certain members is greater than the number of links between those members and others outside. (Thus in Figure 10 the members of sub-group PEQR have more links among themselves than they have to any other member.) The point at which a cluster of members may be called a sub-network or, to put it in a slightly different way, the point at which we can say that a group forms part of a larger network, is established by an arbitrary criterion. We may characterise as sub-networks only those clusters of members who are totally connected with one another, or to clusters consisting of totally connected members plus those other members who have more than an arbitrarily decided minimum of links with the totally connected members. In deciding whether a man belongs to a sub-network or not, we therefore look at the number of his connections with it and compare it to our arbitrary criterion. If we define as a sub-network a cluster whose members have *no* connection with the rest of the network, Figure 11 shows one network. The network is divisible into three if we stipulate that a sub-network must be connected with the main group by not more than one link, and into four if we stipulate that there must be no more than two.

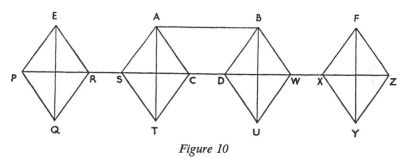

Figure 10

A special case is the network in which highly central members have relatively few links. Some hierarchies are of this type. A hierarchy is defined partly by the content of its communications, such as orders and rewards. It has also certain network peculiarities of which the chief is the fact that the lower centrality-levels have markedly more members than the higher. Since a hierarchy is a very regular symmetric pattern there are also very few centrality-levels relative to the number of members, e.g. in a firm, two thousand people may be distributed between four levels. A hierarchy guards against the too easy disruption of its communication system by encouraging intra-level communication. It will be seen that the hierarchy in Figure 11 is much more easily disrupted than that in Figure 12.

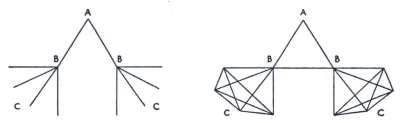

Figures 11 and 12

The centrality figures for patterns 11 and 12 are shown below. It will be noted that in Figure 11, A is the central member. In Figure 12, the two members B are the most central. The additional links in Figure 11 are superfluous in that they do not increase speed of information-transmission. They have the useful function of minimising the chances of disruption.

Table for Figure 11		*Table for Figure 12*	
A	15·5	A	11·4
B	14·7	B	14·7
C	10·0	C	10·3

The member through whom information must flow from one sub-network to another is in the position of an 'open cell'.

ASSUMPTION NINE

Let some members be open to influence and information from the environment.

Through the member in the position of an open cell, information comes to the other members. It now becomes possible to think of the group as surviving in an environment. Every group is and needs to be linked to other groups which are its environment. Thus the group is in the position of a sub-network, adapting itself to the information fed into it from a greater network. After information is fed in through the open cells, the resources of the group are called upon to deal with this information as well as they can. If it is necessary to adapt speedily to the environment it is obviously an advantage to have the important open cells as central as possible, and also to have them closely interdependent, since they may each have access to different parts of the environment. The levels of a hierarchy are also distinguishable in terms of the part of the environment to which they have access.

In practice, for instance when analysing the communication structure of an industrial firm, we specify the type of information we are interested in and neglect all open cells which bring in other kinds of information. Thus it may be important to study the outside contacts of a board of directors and the information that flows into the firm through them, but the telephonist, whose function is also that of an open cell, is taken less seriously.

ASSUMPTION TEN

Let the information spread from a single member in a group differentiated into sub-groups.

This assumption enables us to trace, in a simplified form, the spread of information from one member throughout the group. It is, of course, especially interesting when this member is in the position of an open cell. If we are able to trace the information spread in this way we can reconstruct from it the nature of the network underlying this group. If we construct a graph of the spread of information over time in a totally connected group we shall obviously find that, at the beginning of the time interval needed for transmission, one member

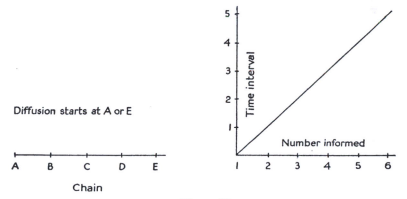

Figure 13

53

has the information, and at the end, all members have it. If the group is organised in a chain (Figure 13) the information diffusion will proceed in arithmetic progression.

If the group is a hierarchy of the type shown in Figure 14 the increase in the numbers informed will be in geometric progression.

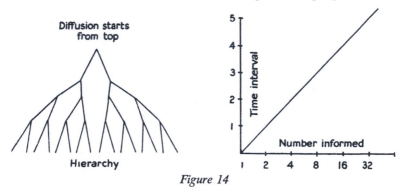

Figure 14

In other types of groups the spread of information is likely to conform to an S-shaped curve (Dodd, 1953). In the first stage the informed member transmits what he knows to those few members who are linked directly to him. These in turn transmit the information to a larger number. A rapid rise in the number of informed persons follows until information comes to reach those members who have already received it from other sources. In this way the number of ignorant members informed decreases. Where several sub-networks overlap, the S-shape might repeat itself several times (Figure 15a). There will be a flattening of the curve when most members of one sub-group are informed, then the links connecting two sub-networks are called into play, and the next nearest sub-group begins to have

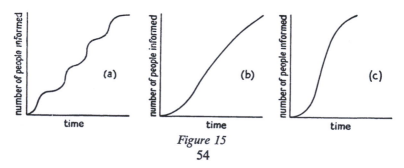

Figure 15

54

the information disseminated through it. One test for overlap of sub-groups might therefore be the 'information-diffusion curve'. The greater the number of links between the sub-networks the less delay there will be in the transmission of information from one network to another, or, the greater are the chances that an uninformed member from another sub-network is contacted. Figures 16 a, b, c, show the kind of network corresponding to the spread of information curves of Figure 15.

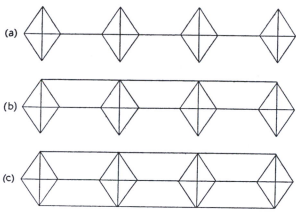

Figure 16

In Figure 16a there is little overlap between the sub-networks, in 16b there is a good deal of overlap, in 16c it is hardly possible to sub-divide the network. Efficiency in communication might therefore be measured in terms of the steepness of the information-diffusion curve, the aim being to get it as steep and straight as possible. The horizontal parts of the curve signify difficulty in transmission at the lower, and superfluity of information at the upper end.

SUMMARY

(1) If all members are alike in all respects, differences in behaviour will be accounted for by the differences between members' positions in the network.

(2) The total possible number of links in a network of n members is $\frac{1}{2}n(n-1)$.

(3) The larger the number of links in a network the greater the number of types of structure that may emerge from the network.

(4) The smaller the sum of all distances between all cells the more information will be spread in one transmission. (All members communicating through all channels at their disposal.)

(5) The smaller the diameter of a network the sooner all members will be completely informed.

(6) For a given number of members and a given number of links between them the speed at which information spreads is shorter with the shorter diameter.

(7) A network in which members differ in centrality index is a differentiated network.

(8) In a differentiated network, where only a limited number of transmissions are permitted, the most central person or subgroup will be the best informed and most influential.

(9) The most central members are in the best position for the correction of errors.

(10) The most central members are most indispensable to the group.

(11) Groups may be distinguished with respect to ease of disintegration.

(12) The system of links in the network differentiates members according to the ease with which they may be cut off from the network.

(13) The spread of information from a single source follows the shape of the S-curve.

(14) The shape of the spread of information curve will show the degree to which sub-groups exist in the group.

(15) Efficiency in communication may be measured by the steepness of the S-curve.

(16) For efficient adaptation to the environment central cells should be open to the environment.

(17) The greater the number of levels of centrality in a network, the greater the advantages the central cells have over others.

CHAPTER FIVE

The Need for Organisation

IN the previous chapter we argued from conditions so remote from social life as we live it that our conclusions, though valid, may seem to have little direct application. Chapter Four was an essay in method; life is more complicated than we supposed in that chapter. People learn, they change, they get in each other's way and have to organise themselves, they are lazy, they want to enjoy themselves, they belong to many groups. It is to such considerations that we must now turn.

Let us consider what we have achieved. We found what kinds of task are best accomplished by co-operation and we have described the group in which skilled men give the orders. Then we saw that skill may become only one among other qualifications for leadership and how this may relate to restricted communication in the group. Lastly, we looked at a method for analysing differences between communication networks. We must now show how different kinds of restricted networks in turn affect the life of the group.

We assume as before that members between them possess all the information needed to solve the problem and that the problem is solved when all possess the total body of knowledge at the disposal of members. Our purpose in this chapter will be to show how the group learns what type of communication system will suit it. We shall consider several related factors. One of these focuses on the efficiency of different communication networks for the solution of group problems, in particular, how a group learns to perform a task in the most efficient way—quickly, in as few steps as possible, accurately, with a quick correction of errors. This means that we must interest ourselves in the organisation of the group. For a group to learn how to perform a task well is to learn how to organise well. There are

57

advantages and disadvantages to the different networks which a group may form. We shall want to examine how a group learns to organise itself in a satisfactory way. There is here an unfortunate gap in our data. On the one hand we could show in Chapter Three how restricted communication comes about in the group. On the other hand we know how and why different networks differ in efficiency. What we cannot prove is that the consequences of different communication networks due to the factors discussed in Chapter Three are similar to the consequences of restricted networks due to the intervention of an experimenter, which we shall discuss here. More experimental work is needed in this area. But it is hoped that this gap will stimulate the reader's imagination. Finally, our discussion of organisation cannot be complete if we do not consider the relation of group efficiency and organisation to what we may call morale factors—the zeal and zest with which members pursue their tasks.

The aims which we have set ourselves make it necessary to modify in some important respects the assumptions used in the previous chapter. The new assumptions will make clear what principles are involved.

ASSUMPTION ONE

Members initially alike may change their function through learning. In the previous chapter our assumption was that all members are inherently alike. Differences in the behaviour of members were to be attributed solely to their position in the network and much trouble was taken not to introduce variables which could not be directly derived from the network in which the members found themselves. The generalisations which were stated as a result were in fact no more than deductions from simple mathematical premises, because it was not only assumed that members were alike but also that they necessarily remained alike. They neither changed nor learned during the group process. That is to say, we were concerned with a static concept of the group. If, however, it is agreed that members may learn and that an antecedent state may influence a succeeding one in other than directly structural ways, a more dynamic model is obtained. Members are therefore now assumed to be alike only at the outset of their experience in the group. Certain of the consequences of the assumption that a member may learn from

58

experience have already been foreshadowed when the spread of information was analysed. We have seen, for instance, how a member's central position in a network determines the experiences to which he is subject during the course of information-transmission: it will be remembered that there are phases in which he possesses more information than the peripheral members. Now it is necessary to work out in detail the more lasting effects of such differences in position.

ASSUMPTION TWO

Let each member communicate to only one other member at a time.
By assuming that each member communicates to only one other member at a time, a factor is introduced into the situation which makes it more difficult for members to understand the nature of the network of which they are a part. They will, therefore, need a good deal of time before they have accumulated sufficient information about the network to communicate directly to those members to which it is most efficient for them to communicate. Indeed, in some networks the links may be so complex that members never learn this at all, and thus never arrive at the stage where they solve a problem in the minimum number of steps. Our new assumption allows us to slow down the learning process sufficiently for us to examine it in detail.[1]

ASSUMPTION THREE

Let us assume that not only information-transmission but also the understanding of messages take time.
The concept of communication used in the previous chapter is so abstract that it can be applied unqualified only in very rare cases. It is not exactly a telephone system; if it were, two people could not communicate simultaneously to one another or to a third without confusion. It is not exactly a postal system; if it were, members who receive a lot of mail would be overworked and hold up other members. What we have so far ignored is the importance of the time factor. Under our present assumptions, the moment that time is introduced as a consideration, organisation becomes of paramount importance. By organisation we mean here a common agreement as to the procedure to be adopted in solving a problem. The group must

[1] See also the discussion at the end of this chapter.

organise if confusion is to be avoided, and if information is to be transmitted in such a way that everyone has something to do and no one has too much to do. In the postal system members must organise in order to avoid boredom or the piling up of messages. The same problem of organisation presents itself in a different guise in the telephone system because you cannot listen to more than one speaker at a time.

ASSUMPTION FOUR

Let the time interval between transmissions be lengthy.

'Lengthy' is an indefinite term. We mean by a lengthy time interval one which avoids the problem of jamming in the postal system by giving the most central member time to deal with all his correspondence before the next lot is allowed to come in. In the telephone system it is a period long enough for everyone to transmit his messages to the recipient of his choice without getting in the way of others who want to communicate to the same person. If we allow a time interval such that even those who receive a lot of information on one occasion have time to assimilate it all, other members may have long periods in which they have nothing to do because they have not received sufficient messages to fill the time. They are bound to get bored.

Let us consider some five-member networks.

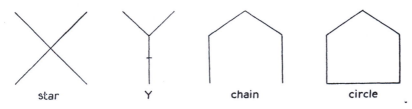

| star | Y | chain | circle |

Figure 1

With these networks Leavitt (1951) conducted the following experiment. Each of five subjects, identified by a colour, was given a card on which appeared a set of five (out of six possible) symbols. Each subject's card was different from all the others in that the symbol lacking, the sixth one, was a different symbol in each case. Thus in any set of five cards there was only one symbol in common.

60

THE NEED FOR ORGANISATION

symbol missing from the hand of :—

	white	red	brown	yellow	blue	common symbol
trial 1	△	◇	✳	○	□	+
trial 2	◇	○	□	△	+	✳
trial 3	+	✳	□	△	◇	○

The problem was for every member to find the common symbol. To accomplish this each member was allowed to communicate, by means of written messages, with those other members of the group to whom he had an open channel (a link in our diagram). He could write to only one other member at a time. A subject who had discovered the answer was allowed to pass the answer along. Messages are sent by members to one another until all have reached a conclusion. This experiment was a very fruitful one. Throughout this chapter we shall refer back to it in relation to its various results. Just now we must focus on the fact that the star, the most efficient network in terms of speed and the lack of errors, was less enjoyed by its members than the circle, the least efficient. The circle is leaderless and no organisation takes place in it; it makes and corrects many errors and is thoroughly enjoyed by its members. It is a network in which there is much confusion, but all members tend to receive the same number of messages. No one will get bored because he has nothing to do. Leavitt also reports that members of the star network said in a later interview that they enjoyed the initial stages of the group more than the later ones. Now in the earlier stages a certain amount of superfluous interaction took place, whereas in the later stages everything was cut and dried for them. In the circle interaction was freer and enjoyment greater: members are less bored.

Action and interaction in a group are enjoyed by the members. Where one man has access to the data which will solve the problem long before the others have it and then communicates the solution to them, he is likely to be the only one to enjoy himself. It is true that Leavitt's group was an experimental one and that performance of the task was as enjoyable for the members as its successful conclusion. Nevertheless, this line of thought may be generalised to less playful situations, such as industrial relations. We may digress to consider this.

First, interaction gives pleasure provided that the task is not so urgent as to outweigh the pleasure of interaction. Where the rapid completion of a number of tasks is the aim of the group, as it might be in industry, enjoyment would have a rather different meaning to members of the group and be more attached to speed and efficiency. Failure would be felt as very frustrating in such a case. But, second, we must remember that morale is likely to be low in departments which have too little to do. For in this case either the members are not persuaded of the importance and urgency of the task and therefore of their own work, or if they are persuaded they feel that the organisation is not making sufficient use of them and they are dissatisfied on those grounds.

People like to exercise their skills. If the communication pattern is such that they cannot, they dislike the situation. Where using one's wits is the real end of the group, the formation of restricted communication-paths either by the experimenter or because of other, social, influences reduces the pleasure taken in the group. This is confirmed by Back (1948) in his study of the interpersonal relations in a discussion group. The barriers to communication in his case were created by the members themselves. Some of them just talked so much that others could not get a word in edgeways. Here also a marked lack of enjoyment was shown by the members deprived of the opportunity to talk when they felt like it.[1] Lastly, the lack of participation of certain members may affect the adaptability of the group (see Assumption Seven).

ASSUMPTION FIVE

Let the time period between transmissions be shortened.

If we shorten the time period in which transmissions are sent we avoid the possibility of boredom. On the other hand, in this case information will pile up at the centre because the central members receive so much information that they cannot assimilate it all before the next batch comes in. Then the problem-solving process is delayed by the bottleneck which the central members have created and the central members are overworked and less likely to function well. If we envisage a telephone system instead of a postal one, and do not arrange for long periods of transmission, three people may all trans-

[1] See also page 103.

mit to a fourth at the same time and cacophony will be the result. This is one way of describing disturbances in communication.

ASSUMPTION SIX

Let there be disturbances in the communication network.

In the previous chapter it was assumed that these disturbances were so grave that communication was not possible because a link was broken. One may, however, postulate disturbances which make communication difficult but not impossible, although, paradoxically indeed, we shall find that it would have been better for the efficiency of the group if the link in which communication is disturbed had been totally destroyed. Disturbances in communication make the co-operative performance of a task more difficult. We shall show that the more important the organisational aspect of the task is, the more difficult it will be to carry on when the communication network is disturbed. (This generalisation is not necessarily true for the case in which communication links are missing rather than difficult to use.)

(a) Let us first take a task which it is possible and easy to carry out alone. The construction of a number of anagrams from a given word is a good example. We have shown in a previous chapter that in such cases the individual product is often better than the group product. We may now venture a reason for this: where information is not perfectly clear and unambiguous more time is spent in solving the problem of what the other member means than on the problem in hand.

Heise and Miller (1951) constructed a number of three-person networks, in which the members communicated through microphone and earphones. The experimenters could introduce into the hearing apparatus noise in controllable amounts, they could, that is to say, introduce as many *decibels* of noise as they wanted to. Although they produced difficulty in understanding by mechanical means, it is easy to see how misunderstanding may be socially induced. Members who are not accustomed to communicate with one another, for instance, and do not know one another, may be confused by one another's idiom or distracted by the effort to get to know each other, which may be more interesting to them than the task is. When members perform best alone, the nature of the network, or the introduction of noise into it, is not likely to make much difference to the group result. For this reason all the networks illustrated below did roughly equally well, and the introduction of greater or lesser intensities of noise through the microphones made no difference either.

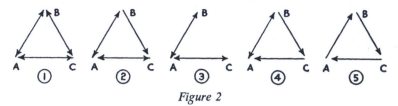

Figure 2

An arrow pointing to member B from member A signifies that A can speak to B, i.e. B can hear A speaking to him but not *vice versa*. Members could speak whenever they wanted to. Some members might therefore be in the unfortunate position of hearing one person speak to their right ear while another was speaking to their left!

(b) A second task which Heise and Miller set their subjects was the re-assembly into one list of three separate lists of words, one being possessed by each member. An example will make the task clear.

Complete list	A's list	B's list	C's list
south			
		south	south
though	though	though	
off	off		
quiz	off		plod
grade	quiz		sniff
act	quiz		pounce
dwarf	grade	grade	rash
plod		act	gun
sniff	act		gun
pounce	dwarf		coast
rash	dwarf		coast
gun	plod		pig
coast		pig	
pig	&c., &c.	sin	
sin		whiff	whiff
whiff		&c., &c.	pent
pent			
&c., &c.			&c., &c.

64

As A reads off a word from his list, the others check to see if it also appears on theirs. If it does they read out the word following A's word. In this way the complete list is reassembled. The order of good performance, of the networks illustrated on page 64 was, in descending order of quality: 1, 3, 2, 4, 5.

How may we account for this result? It is gratifying to find we can account for it in its entirety. An examination of the networks will show that there are two kinds of disturbance to which the members were subject. One is the noise mentioned above; the other is a disturbance to which network 2 rather than either network 1 or 3 is subject. It is the fact that member B interrupts member C. The introduction of extraneous noise makes any communication which is not mutual a hindrance rather than a help. In network 2, member B has a choice as to whom to communicate with and when he chooses C instead of A, C has to waste precious time in order to correct him through A. And if B speaks to C at the same time as A, C has to tell A to ask B to be quiet! Accordingly we find that network 2 is slower than either network 1 or 3. It is for this reason that we said on page 63 the link was better destroyed than disturbed. In network 5 there is no direct communication between any two members. If A wants to check on what B said, he has to use C as an intermediary. This enlarges the possibilities of misunderstandings. All the other networks were more efficient than this one. Of the remainder, all except network 4 have more than one link through which mutual communication may pass. Network 4 is accordingly the next least efficient. To sum up so far: when two members cannot communicate mutually, the communication of the one to the other is likely to act as a disturbance and not as a help. Because in this way all messages may be delayed, both the performance of the task and the efficient organisation of the group will be more difficult in networks of this kind.

In this way we may explain another finding of Leavitt's. In the experiment already quoted on page 60 the members communicated to only one other at a time. Since they had no knowledge of the network they must have chosen the members to whom they communicated in a random fashion. Now random communications are more likely to be mutual in some networks than in others. Obviously, the smaller the number of choices at the disposal of members the more likely it is that they will hit on a mutual communication. In a two-member group, for instance, if both members communicate they must do so mutually; they have no choice. Conversely, the greater the number of links between the members, the slower the spread of information is likely to be, because members' choices will be less restricted and the probability of a mutual communication will decline.[1] Let us now consider Leavitt's networks again.

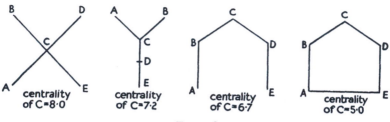

Figure 3

It will be seen that the star has four members who have no choice as to whom they shall communicate with, it has to be the central member; the 'Y' has three such members; the chain two and the circle none at all. Therefore the sequence from most to least efficient should be star—'Y'—circle—chain. The results are not quite as clear as one would wish; nevertheless out of a series of fifteen trials, the fastest single trial was attained by the star, the next by the 'Y', and so on.

Mutuality of communication obviously helps the group to perform efficiently. One reason we have shown is that if two members do communicate simultaneously to a third, one of them can be asked to wait. No intermediary is necessary to transmit that (organisational) message. Second, if A has sent information to B which contradicts B's store of knowledge it can be cleared up very much more easily if the two can inform each other directly of the existence of the discrepancy than if this correction has to be mediated by a third. Learning depends directly on the possibility of correcting errors. The greater the possibilities of error, the more important such feedbacks become. This is true both for learning information which is available through others and also for learning which channels of communication must be used in order to arrive speedily at a solution. Third, in a network in which there is a mutual link between some members and not between others, members differ in centrality. The more central members have more information sent to them or through them than

---

[1] This discussion is taken up again at the end of the present chapter.

other members. They are therefore in a better position for spotting discrepancies in information sent from two different sources and they can co-ordinate the efforts of others. We shall see from the next experiment that co-ordination may be very important. Lastly, we know that the central member may reach a solution before other members do so. If he then transmits the solution through the network the group as a whole possesses the solution; they need not each wait for all messages to reach them—a valuable saving of time.

(c) A third task performed in the networks constructed by Heise and Miller was complicated and for good performance there had to be a member who would co-ordinate the efforts of the group. Twenty-five words were distributed between the three members, who were required to construct a sentence out of them. Quite clearly the structure of the group affects the perceptions of the members as to the role they are best fitted to fulfil in the circumstances. Perception of the existence of leadership differs in the various networks and it differs in accordance with the centrality indices of the members. In groups where it is easy for members to perceive that there is a co-ordinator, they are likely to make use of his offices and thus speed up the performance of the task. In Leavitt's experiment the order for the fastest single solution, taken out of a series of fifteen trials, was: star—'Y'—chain—circle. The centrality indices of the most central member for these patterns are: 8·0—7·2—6·7—5·0 respectively. The more central the central member therefore, the more efficient the group. The central member turns easily into a co-ordinator and this is important if the task is complicated. It is because the highly central member is easily recognised as the 'natural' co-ordinator that patterns with marked centrality-differences do well.[1] In the others, although all members may recognise the need for co-ordination, they have to devote more time to a discussion of organisational procedure in order to appoint a co-ordinator. This hypothesis is corroborated by an experiment quoted by Bavelas (1952). Members of three types of networks were asked if their group had a leader, after the group had performed tasks very like those described above. (It is interesting to find that no one asked what the experimenter meant by 'leader'.) The three networks are shown in Figure 4.

[1] Here again we find evidence that interaction necessitated by the task is enjoyed. The co-ordinating position, i.e. the one which receives direct communications from the other members, was very much preferred by the members to the peripheral positions.

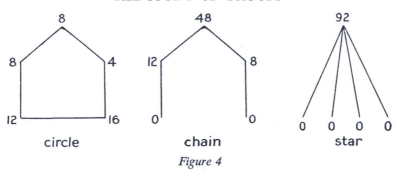

circle   chain   star

Figure 4

The figures stand for the percentage of responses which indicate a leader by position in the network. As is to be expected, the circle members don't know and their guesses are pretty equally distributed among all positions. The central members of the chain and star are frequently, and the peripheral members never, perceived to be in a leadership position. Christie, Macy and Luce (1952, p. 177) also submit evidence that a central member of the chain network deduces from the number and type of messages that he gets that he must be in the central position. Accordingly we find in the Heise and Miller experiment that networks in which the centralities of all members are equal did not encourage the emergence of this function. In network 3, A is the most central member and the natural co-ordinator. Accordingly we find that network 3 is more rapid and accurate than network 1.

ASSUMPTION SEVEN

Let there be a change of routine in the history of the group.
The evidence so far leads us to believe that a group with mutuality of communication and a clearly recognisable central member as co-ordinator are best suited to solve problems in which each member possesses information useful to others and which are so complex that a co-ordinator is required. The ease with which a routine can be established is obviously very important. Routine reduces the organisational difficulties of the group. Members do not have to decide for themselves and therefore do not delay the group in making up their minds as to whom they ought to be communicating with. Thus they can get on with the task of communicating their information. Such a routine is established quite easily with a highly

restricted communication structure in which communication is mutual and in which there is one highly central member. In corroboration of this hypothesis we may quote Leavitt's finding that a routine was established very soon in the star, in the 'Y' a little later, in the chain later again, and in the circle never; the speed of problem solving in these networks varied in the same order.

There are, however, dangers in such organisation. Routine means that members become used to performing a task in a certain way. Suppose now the task changes half-way through the experiment. A number of experiments were run along these lines. In some of them the uncertainty was introduced by the means used by Heise and Miller, i.e., by interference with the communication channels. In others the task was initially that of finding which of a set of marbles the five members possessed was common to all members. After this problem had been solved fifteen times, a new set of marbles was used which were cloudy or ambiguous in colour, so that there were difficulties in describing precisely the shade of one's marbles, and in deciding whether one's own greenish blue marble was the same as someone else's turquoise or peacock. The experimenters (Christie, Macy and Luce, 1952–53) ran their experiments apparently in the hope that they would be able to estimate the effect of 'noise' or 'uncertainty' or 'ambiguity' on the performance of tasks in different networks.

In effect, however, their results show some interesting consequences of rigid structuring or wrong learning. If very similar tasks are performed a number of times and then the nature of the task changes, what results can we predict? All that we know seems to point firmly to the hypothesis that the circle will do better than the chain and the chain than the star. Let us examine the evidence. First, the better a routine has been learned, the more reward its rigid keeping has brought in the past, the less willing will members be to abandon it now that they are uncertain and in stress. They will not be able or willing to recognise that the change in the nature of the task involves a change in the structure of the group. (See also Homans, 1950, p. 102.)

Second, the members in the circle have been enjoying themselves. They have been participating actively. In the star on the other hand, there are four members and in the chain two, who have had nothing to do but to send out information at their disposal and then wait for the correct answer to come back to them. The members in the circle are therefore more strongly motivated to perform their task with zest. In the other two networks, members have learned to sit back and to leave the thinking to the central members. It is nothing to them that they now leave the central member in a mess. Third, let us look at the networks again.

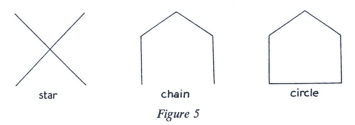

star   chain   circle

Figure 5

In the star the central member now gets ambiguous or even contradictory information and no one else gets any information. Therefore even if the central member asks 'What do you mean by "yellowish"?' there is nothing in the experience of the peripheral member that will enable him either to interpret the reason for this question or to place it within a range of yellowishness and its shadings into browns, reds or greens. In the circle there are sufficient interconnections for everyone to realise that something odd is going on. Since everyone transmits everyone else's messages, there is sufficient information at the disposal of members for them to sort things out, if necessary each for himself. Moreover, the circle members tend in any case to send more organisational messages than do other networks (Leavitt, 1951), and to arrive at all kinds of short cuts. If they have learned anything at all, it is how to cope with uncertainty (Leavitt: Bavelas in *Cybernetics*, 1952).

Similarly with the correction of errors. In normal conditions, without noise or ambiguity, errors in the star are corrected by the central member or not at all. Other members cannot get a chance to learn to do this. In the same conditions everyone in the circle has practice in checking items of information against one another. Leavitt has shown that the members of the circle learned to correct many of the great number of errors they made. They did not correct many to begin with, but they learned to do so as the trials proceeded. This learning also is carried over to the new situation. The star and the chain are less adept at the reduction of error, having had less practice in doing so on their previous task.

NOTE TO CHAPTER FIVE

At first sight the reader may wonder at the unrealism of the conditions in which the experiments quoted in this and the previous chapter were carried on. He may doubt whether the findings based on them are at all likely to be useful in understanding human behaviour. To this question there are two replies. The first may be dealt with briefly. Some of our findings are directly useful in the analysis of small group processes. Perhaps among these are those on the restriction of communication in Chapter Three, and those related to routine and to organisation in the present chapter.

The second aspect must be dealt with a little more fully. Properly speaking, this subject deserves a book to itself. Granted that in small groups the members can usually all speak to one another, can choose whom they will speak to or not speak to, do not need intermediaries to communicate to other members, do not perform the same tasks over and over again, do not form routines, etc. etc., there are important situations where these conditions do obtain. They obtain in any large organisation. Many of the experiments we have outlined throw light on the processes operating in large organisations.

Let us take as a first example our assumption that a man communicates to only one other in a group at a time. It cannot apply to people conversing in a group or to the kind of large organisation in which memoranda are sent to all members at a certain level or in a certain section. But the assumption fits a very interesting case. People belong to more than one group. Several groups may be in contact with one another because they have a member in common. This member can transmit information from one group to the other. He may be a node in the *informal* communication system of a large organisation. Suppose that two groups are working independently of one another and that each group has information which would be useful to the other group. Suppose that neither group realises this. Suppose now that group A has a member *a* with a link to member *b* in group B. There is then potentially a channel of communication between the two groups. But *a* and *b* each have links to many other groups and they may not realise for some time that they might be

71

useful to one another. Or suppose that *a* and *b* do not know one another, but are the only members of groups A and B who are at all likely to meet. This is very like assuming that the network of the group in which a member can communicate to only one other member at a time is a totally connected one and that the choice as to who shall be the recipient of a communication, is, at least at first, randomly determined.

This is the first step by which a structure emerges out of a network, or an informal organisation out of a formal one. Obviously there are only a limited number of structures that can emerge by this process from a totally connected network of a given number of members. Thus, for instance, for a three-person group the potential connection can only be either:

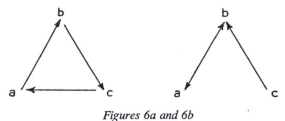

Figures 6a and 6b

For a four-person group there are six different possible structures.

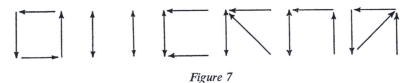

Figure 7

The number of structures for a group of *n* members is factorial $(n - 1)$. For a five-person group the number of possible structures would therefore be $4 \times 3 \times 2 = 24$. We will not attempt to show them all (Leeman, 1952).

The patterns shown above are assumed to be structures after the first transmission of information and we have stated that members are initially alike. Though they may change with experience, the first transmission takes place before they have learned. For this reason the following two structures are the same:

Similarly the following four structures are also identical:

If a man does not know the nature of the network in which he is placed, his choice as to whom he will approach with or for information may be made on a more or less random basis. Certainly we cannot easily predict his choice. We are now considering a group which is potentially totally connected, i.e. each member may talk to any other member, as, for instance, at a cocktail party or within the informal system of a large organisation. Experimentally the group is one in which members send out messages through a channel at their disposal and hope to receive a message in return, an assumption which we have already used in this chapter.

Suppose that *b* has information useful to *c*, and that the reverse is not the case. Then *c* will approach *b*, but *b* will not necessarily respond. In that case we have a link which can be said to be in one direction only, not mutual. Or suppose that *b* is a go-between for *a* and *c*, rewarded by *a* if he transmits information from *c*, but not by *c* for a similar service. This is another case in which information-transmission will not be mutual. The channels of communication will then be those of Figure 6b. Or a situation may arise in which *a* is prepared to be useful to *b* because *b* can make *c* useful to *a* (Figure 6a). This situation may be made to apply to groups in an organisation as well as to members of a group, in the following way. Suppose *a* has a link with *b* who is of no use to group A except that he has a link with *c* in group C, and *c* is useful. How likely is it that groups A and C will become aware of the fact that interaction between them would be to their mutual advantage?

It will be seen that in some structures illustrated in Figure 7 there has been one mutual communication, in others two, and in one

73

structure none. It can be shown that if a group is to perform a task in the fewest possible number of steps, in the conditions assumed here, it must at first transmission have hit on the largest number of mutual communications. The proof is complicated and will not be further discussed here.[1] The empirical verification of this condition has already been given by the experiments quoted on pages 65–66.

Plainly the probability that a large number of mutual communications will come about by chance at first transmission is very small in a totally connected group. The number of choices open to a member is too great. The fewer the number of links open to members of a group the more restricted their choice and the larger the probability of a mutual choice occurring.

SUMMARY

(1) The number of structures that can emerge after one random transmission in a totally connected network of n members is factorial $(n - 1)$.

(2) If a group is to perform the task in the fewest possible steps, it must at first transmission have hit on the largest possible number of mutual links.

(3) The smaller the number of choices at the disposal of members, the more likely it is that they will hit on a mutual communication.

(4) The smaller the number of choices at the disposal of members:
(a) the quicker the problem is solved;
(b) the more easily errors are corrected;
(c) the smaller the number of errors made;

---

[1] See, however, Christie, Luce and Macy, pp. 61 ff. Notice how important knowledge of the whole network is in a group with subgroups. In the network here illustrated each member communicates with only one other at a time, and members are assumed to be unaware of the structure of their group. The chances are that quite a number of transmissions would have to occur before the information at the disposal of A, C, D is transmitted to B, E, F, G. Errors due to lack of information in either subgroup are therefore unlikely to be corrected.

(d) the more easily the organisation of the network is perceived by the members;

(e) the less the peripheral members have to do and the less they enjoy themselves.

(5) Disturbances in the network affect groups engaged in solving a task which needs a high degree of organisation, more than other groups.

(6) A change in routine disrupts a highly organised group more than other groups because:

(a) they have learned their routine more perfectly;

(b) peripheral members are less strongly motivated to do well;

(c) they have had less practice in correcting errors;

(d) they have no access to data for comparative purposes;

(e) less highly organised groups tend to be used to sending organisational messages as well as messages that are task-related.

(7) Mutuality of communication ensures that:

(a) 'noise' created by an interrupting member can be quickly dealt with;

(b) organisational messages can be rapidly transmitted;

(c) messages concerning the task itself can be rapidly transmitted;

(d) mistakes due to faulty transmission can be easily cleared up;

(e) the problem of co-ordination is simplified.

(8) Marked differences in the centralities of members allow the central member to be easily perceived as co-ordinator. The central member will also reach a solution (whether correct or not) before other members and can transmit his solution to them. This shortens the time needed by the group to solve its problem.

CHAPTER SIX

The Evolution of Norms

W E must now deal with an aspect of group life that we have so far been able to take for granted. Members interacting in a group develop sentiments: feelings about one another, about the work they are doing, about many other things. Implicit in such sentiments is a ranking in terms of preference: one end being preferred to another, this means to that, this person to the next. Although such preferences may be related to one another in a very complex way, and may even be inconsistent with one another at times, they do lead a man to make evaluations, comparisons between persons, or things, or actions, in terms of a better and a worse. Festinger and his associates (1954) have called this process the 'social comparison process' and have studied it in great detail.[1] We shall touch on it only in so far as it relates to our own argument in this and subsequent chapters.

Whether a man will evaluate his own actions and those of other people as better or as worse, whether he will approve of an action or a proposed course of action depends on a whole system of values, on his physical, social and moral frame of reference. This frame is composed of 'norms'—actions or actors are evaluated by reference to the individual's norms. This means that we use the word 'norms' in a rather wider sense than is customary, but we shall define our use carefully so that although our concept may be wide it shall not be loose. By an individual's set of norms we mean all the standards, whether practical or moral, which lead him to rank one man or one action as preferable to another in a given set of circumstances. Norms are of very great influence on individual behaviour. We shall

[1] The study here referred to is a most important one; no students of small groups can ignore it. Although their argument is not used by us, a great deal of use has been made of this work in the present and other chapters. The debt is most gratefully acknowledged.

76

see that they affect variables which have until recently been regarded as the prerogative of general psychology, such variables as perception, judgement, level of aspiration and competitiveness.

Norms are acquired through the interactions of persons. They are learned. This learning process may be briefly sketched on the following lines.

The individual's first experience of life is within the family. By being born into this group he is conditioned in many ways to seek out others for the satisfaction of his needs; as a consequence he will need to live his life in the context of small groups of others. The attainment of his own desires—either for companionship or for other gratifications—will depend on the extent to which he can induce others to co-operate with him. This in turn depends on the extent to which he can please them or gain their support. When in a group a man will consider his actions with respect to others in the group. He learns to conform to their expectations and so to their way of life. Their ways have value for the individual, he may make them his own, internalise them and therefore conform to them. Or they may be experienced as external pressures to which he must yield to gain other ends. Such pressures, whether internalised or not, we are calling norms. 'A norm, then, is an idea in the minds of the members of the group, an idea that can be put in the form of a statement specifying what the members or other men should do or ought to do, are expected to do, under given circumstances.' (Homans, 1950, p. 123.)

In tracing the development of norms we shall see that on becoming established they affect the behaviour of members of the group as though they were independent variables. Although they do so, we need not suppose the existence of any kind of 'group mind'.

'Let us make the matter clear once again. If a Psychology, concerned with exploring the predispositions, the instincts, the motives and the aims of an individual man down to his actions and his relations with those who are nearest to him, had completely achieved its task, and had cleared up the whole of these matters with their interconnections, it would then suddenly find itself confronted by a new task which would lie before it unachieved. It would be obliged to explain the surprising fact that under a certain condition this individual whom it had come to understand thought, felt, and acted in quite a different way from what would have been expected. And this condition is his insertion into a collection of people which has acquired the characteristic of a "psychological group". What, then, is a "group"? How does it acquire the capacity for exercising such a decisive influence over the mental life of the individual? And what is the nature of the mental change which it forces upon the individual?' (Freud, 1921; Strachey translation 1949, pp. 5, 6.)

As Freud formulates the problem, it seems an insoluble one. The reason for this lies in the too sharp distinction he draws between individual and society. If the problem is formulated in a different way, it disappears. It should cause no surprise that an individual changes his behaviour when he enters a group; current theory may be too general to be useful for precise experimental work, but it is quite adequate to account for this. When relationships between the individual and his social environment are considered, one is in fact analysing the effect of placing a system that is apparently in isolation—the individual—within a larger system—the group—and thus subjecting it to the forces operating within the larger system. At this very abstract level one may distinguish between situations in which the forces within the previously isolated system are reinforced, or redirected, or inhibited, by the forces now directed upon it from outside. The difficulty lies, as always, in identifying the circumstances in which one or other of these effects occurs, but at least we are not faced with an insoluble problem.

The norms which govern the individual's behaviour are inevitably group-related: the individual has learned to perceive his situation in terms of previous experiences which seem to him to have elements significantly similar to his present position. The more easily he perceives this similarity, the more relevant certain norms appear and therefore the greater the pressure upon him to behave in accordance with them. The recognition of similarity gives the situation its meaning for him and removes uncertainty. The more remote the similarity, the more difficult it is for the individual to recognise the specific norms with which his behaviour should accord. In this chapter we examine the consequences for the individual of the degree to which he is able to take specific norms of specific groups into consideration. The degree to which he is able to do this will obviously depend on the information at the disposal of the individual, information about the norms of the group in which he finds himself, or information about the relevance of previously learned norms to his present situation.

We begin with a situation in which the individual finds it difficult to choose norms which are relevant to his position.

ASSUMPTION ONE

Let the individual work alone, at a task unfamiliar to him.

When an individual is working alone, there is no way in which he can compare his own performance with that of others. In an unfamiliar situation he cannot use his previous experience of other people in setting a standard for his own performance. In such an undefined situation there is no single group available to limit his behaviour in specific ways. The norms of many groups might be relevant to his problem. Unless he belongs to a group to which he is so strongly attached that its norms affect all of his behaviour, the effect of multiple group membership will be to emphasise those values for the individual which appear in all the groups he knows.[1] The more or less common denominators will have the greatest effect on him and in this way the individual will find himself subject to culture-wide pressures. In our culture, the most striking of these common denominators is *success*.

A man wants to distinguish himself. But in the condition we have assumed he does not know how to set about it. According to Festinger (1954) 'in the absence of both a physical and a social comparison, subjective evaluations of opinions and abilities are unstable.' The man does not know at what point his performance of a task will be noted as remarkable. He could try to stand out either as noticeably better than others, or as noticeably worse. As a rule he will try for the former, since anyone can perform badly but not everyone can perform well. Still, any schoolteacher can give examples of children who, unable to stand out by good performances, distinguish themselves by outrageously bad behaviour.

Wherever the behaviour of the individual comes under review this striving to acquit himself well has to be taken into account as an explanatory variable. It is, of course, specially relevant to studies of

---

[1] Cf. T. Parsons' pattern variables, in particular the dimension *specificity–diffuseness*.

competitiveness, since the striving for success is best characterised by competition. It is interesting to note, since it confirms our hypothesis, that in the absence of positive encouragement *not* to compete, sets of individuals tend to structure the situation competitively. Sprott (1952) comments on the difficulty Whittemore (1924) encountered in restraining the competitive spirit when individuals are working in proximity with one another:

'Whittemore, making use of a rubber stamp printing task, tried to compare the competitive situation with the non-competitive one by telling the subjects not to compete. The most significant result of this investigation was that it revealed how difficult it was to avoid competition entirely. Gradually and almost imperceptibly it asserted itself, usually with deleterious results on the quality of the work done.'

Sengupta and Sinha (1926) also report that the performance of individuals speeds up when they work within sight of one another. The sight of others at work seems sufficient to set in motion the need to compete. Dashiell (1930), to whom we shall refer again in the next few pages, makes a very similar point. He suggests increasing performance scores along the continuum: working alone without knowledge that others are performing the same tasks—working alone with that knowledge—working in rivalry with others.[1]

The more aware the individual is of the presence of others, the more effort he will make to acquit himself well. Up to a limit which will be analysed below, the effort will show itself in a striving for a very good performance.

ASSUMPTION TWO

Let the group be present and let its norms be unknown to the individual newly placed in it.

This situation is only slightly different from the one assumed above. The subject is still assumed to be ignorant of the specific norms of the group and therefore largely ignorant of the appropriate behaviour. But the group is present; he can actually see its members; he is more aware of it than he was before. We may say that it is

---

[1] The material on which we have drawn in this chapter comes from a very well documented field. Dashiell's (1930) study is another meticulous and erudite contribution to small group theory. This debt also is gratefully acknowledged.

psychologically 'nearer' and this should give an added impetus to his efforts. It is therefore reasonable to postulate that if he is given a task and allowed to perform it in front of the group to demonstrate his skill, his performance will improve. An audience is just such a group.

Travis (1925) studied the effects of a small audience on the performance of a simple hand-eye co-ordination task. The subject had to touch a spot on a moving target with a rod. He knew nothing of the standards of the audience, the audience did not communicate with the subject. It was simply present. The subject had had previous trials with his task and had reached a stage where his performance was not improving with further practice. Under the relatively mild stimulus of the audience, eighteen out of the twenty-two subjects improved on their best previous scores. If success is valued, the opportunity to demonstrate one's skill acts as a stimulus to good performance.

It is to be noted that the interaction between the individual and the group is very limited and therefore the directions in which performance may vary is limited also. The subject knew nothing about his audience and had merely deduced from earlier experience that he is likely to rise in their esteem if he performs well. The audience, however, will not be able to judge skill in all aspects of the task. One may reason from this that the aspects of the task on which the individual will perform best under observation are those in which he can most easily be seen to be successful.

ASSUMPTION THREE

Let some aspects of the task be more easily evaluated than others.
In this situation the individual is still very largely ignorant of the norms of his audience. He has, however, some information about the task and this will influence his performance of it.

Dashiell's subjects engaged in tasks like multiplication, mixed relations and serial association (1930). After their performance when alone had been noted by the experimenter, the subjects continued on similar tasks closely watched by one or two observers who sat beside them or stood over them during their performance. Under such close observation the subjects worked more rapidly, though not more accurately, than before. Taking this result together with Travis', one may easily see that our hypothesis is correct. Subjects under close

G   81

supervision improve most markedly in those aspects of the task which are most obvious to the observer. In Travis' test a buzz could be heard when a mistake was made; the subject therefore had a strong incentive towards accuracy. In Dashiell's test it was not obvious to the observer whether the subject's performance was correct or not, but only how quickly he got through the task; hence speed increased.

ASSUMPTION FOUR

Let the individual take part in a competitive situation.

In competitive situations the individual is intensely aware of the presence of others.

By introducing the element of competition explicitly, the group is induced to bring more pressure to bear on the individual, but the pressure is still very general; no specific information about the group's norms is as yet available. In rivalry situations the group may or may not be physically present. This hardly matters. What is important is that the individual is put under additional stress by a group. As he performs his task he is under continuous pressure to perform well. He is continually watching himself and comparing himself with some other group. Little wonder that once again those aspects of the work which can be most easily evaluated receive special attention. Usually speed is increased at the expense of accuracy. Thus a further finding of Dashiell's (1930) shows that rivalry increases speed as much as an audience of onlookers does. If the performer were as much aware of his accuracy as of his speed he would improve that aspect as well. That this is a justifiable hypothesis is shown by Hurlock's (1927) experiment in which an arithmetic class improved throughout the week until it was 40 per cent above the control group in speed, and, unlike Dashiell's group, improved somewhat in accuracy as well. Speed the children could judge for themselves; it improved remarkably. Accuracy was brought into their situation because the results of one test were made known before the next, but because it was not so directly present to their minds at the time of performance it was rather less influential. Studies of the performance of co-operative groups when compared to competitive ones confirm these results. The co-operative group is more accurate, more thorough, but slower (Deutsch, 1949).[1]

[1] See also our discussion on competition on p. 34.

Let the individual perform a task with other members of the group.
So far it has been shown that the more closely an individual is
aware of the group the more ardently he will strive for a good performance. There is, however, a limit to this relationship. We arrived
at our generalisations concerning success by assuming the possible
reference groups to be so remote that no values besides success are
clearly discernible; now we shall assume that the interaction between
the group and the individual is of a more concrete type. He can
watch their performance and they can watch his. When a group is
sufficiently close to the individual for him to know some of its norms,
he is likely to strive for success in very specific ways. At the beginning
of this chapter it was argued that to belong to a group means to conform to its values and that to seek for membership obliges the individual to solicit approval by such conformity. The greater the individual's knowledge of the group, the more precise the direction
which his search for approval will take. When a member can watch
the performance of others he has more adequate information on the
kind of performance that will be appreciated. Similarly, if an experimenter gives information concerning the group and its values,
the individual will be able to estimate within a narrower range than
before what kind of performance will be most acceptable. There are,
for instance, performances which are *too* good, so good that they
make the performance of others appear unsuccessful by comparison.
The literature of industrial sociology affords many opportunities for
studying the difficulties under which the 'rate buster' labours (Roy,
1952, Dalton, 1948). It must be remembered that good performance
is not an end, according to our argument, but a means toward being
accepted by a valued group. After all, what the individual wants is
the appreciation of those he values: for this reason he will conform
to their expectations. If they don't work hard, why should he?

The aspiring member who desires to belong to a group will observe
the kind of behaviour current in the group and he will seek to imitate
it. The striving for success, for distinguished performance, may thus
be inhibited by the need to establish membership and the aspiring
member will be careful to behave like the other members of the
group. Since it is easier to conform to observed behaviour than to
infer from current practices what the ideal may be, the behaviour of

the new member will be regulated by the *average* performance of the group, which may or may not be the *ideal*. His ignorance will lead him to conform to the most easily observed behaviour rather than to that which is more nearly ideal and therefore less frequently observed. In this way, one may account for the curious way in which extremes in individual behaviour 'level out' in the group and become much less marked.

Dashiell (1930) quotes a good deal of evidence that the group has a levelling effect. Thus, for instance, he recounts an experiment of Allport's (1924) which shows that the presence of co-workers increases speed of performance, which is attributable to the greater psychological nearness of the group, and that, moreover, the slower workers are more affected by this pressure than fast workers. Lorenz (1933) is also mentioned as noting that fast workers tend to slow down in a group and slow workers speed up. (The slow workers speed up more than the fast ones slow down.) The effect of working in a group is thus shown to be a reduction of the range of deviations round a mean.

The group is a pacemaker; individuals regulate their effort according to what they perceive to be happening in the rest of the group. The earlier psychologists have tended to explain the improved performance of slow workers in terms of increased motivation provided by the presence of other people. This explanation takes no account of the fact that fast workers tend to slow down when working in a group. A better explanation would be in terms of the increased information which the group affords the individual. The group provides a frame of reference for the individual's judgement. A man finds out how much work is expected of one in his situation and behaves accordingly. This is very neatly demonstrated by an experiment made by Chapman and Volkmann (in Newcomb *et al.*, 1952). Students were asked how many questions in a general knowledge paper they thought they would be able to answer correctly. The subjects were given spurious information concerning the performance of other groups, which were alleged to be authors and literary critics for one group, and W.E.A. students for another. All subjects were given the same score but some were led to believe that the authors obtained this score and others that it was the score of the W.E.A. students. They were then asked again how well they expected to do themselves. They changed their levels of aspiration, i.e. their norms,

84

markedly after the additional information was given them, those who had been given the score of the higher group (authors) lowering, and those who had been given the score of the lower group (W.E.A.) increasing their own estimate.

The conclusion at which we arrive through all this evidence is that the striving for extreme scores is characteristic of men ignorant of the norms of the group or isolated from the group. This is well documented in sociological literature under the heading of *anomie*. When a man can place himself in a group and introject its values, he will be able to regulate his behaviour by what is normal for that group. He will strive to do well in the role allotted to him.[1]

ASSUMPTION SIX

Let the individual perform a task with other members of the group, when no one is in a position to evaluate his own performance or that of other members.

Festinger (1954) makes a very valuable distinction between physical and social comparisons. In the former type of comparison, the individual can evaluate his own situation by more or less objective indices. In the latter, he must base his evaluation on the opinion of others.

'In many instances, perhaps most, whether or not an opinion is correct cannot be immediately determined by reference to the physical world. . . . One could, of course, test the opinion that an object was fragile by hitting it with a hammer, but how is one to test that a certain political candidate is better than another, or that war is inevitable? . . . To the extent that objective physical bases

[1] Three further comments may be made on the individual's conformity to group norms. Firstly, conformity may be restricted to those norms which are of importance to the group. Schachter (1951) reports that the pressure to conform is much less strong in groups in which a topic is being discussed that does not seriously interest the members. Before he constructed his groups he asked his subjects which of a number of topics they were anxious to discuss. He gratified the wishes of some and put others into groups discussing topics for which they had not opted. In the former groups the deviant members experienced a good deal more pressure to conform than in the latter.

Secondly, Homans reports that pressure to conform may vary with the status of the members. A group may recognise that a leader has functions which make it necessary for him to conform less strongly to the norms of the group.

Thirdly, it is not to be expected that the individual values all groups equally. Within the limits of his capacity, the individual can choose to which norms he will aspire. This issue may be confused by the fact that sometimes a group deliberately aspires to approximate in some respects to the behaviour of favoured out-group individuals like film-stars.

85

for evaluation are not available, subjective judgements of correct or incorrect opinion and subjectively accurate assessments of one's ability depend on how one compares with other persons.'

Under our previous assumption, we discussed the case in which the individual had an unambiguous physical basis for comparison. He could see how much others in the group were producing and regulate his own performance accordingly. The situation was subjective in Festinger's sense only in so far as the individual relied on group norms in judging whether a performance was 'good' or 'bad'. His moral frame or reference was influenced by the group, his physical frame of reference was determined by a situation which left little room for ambiguity.[1]

Sometimes, however, the physical frame of reference is inadequate and ambiguous. When this is so, the individual can perceive the situation in a number of different ways and his perception will be much influenced by his own needs, moods, and expectations. When the individual lacks knowledge of fact and is called upon to act, he will seize whatever hints he can elicit from the environment, physical or social. Where his only source of knowledge is the opinion of others, he can use only information thus obtained and by this means he may take for fact what is no more than consensus of opinion. In such a situation, the power of the group over the individual is most marked. Two factors therefore determine the influence of the group: the amount of information the individual has at his disposal independently of the group, and the psychological reality or pressure of the group. Many workers have produced situations in which the individual's frame of reference is very inadequate. Therefore, any information which will structure the situation is likely to have a very great influence on the individual. Some examples will make the process clear.

Consider the voting behaviour of individuals in a situation where they know really nothing about the candidates for whom they are asked to vote. In such a case, any information which will provide a limit to the possibilities which have to be considered will be eagerly seized upon. In an experiment by Festinger (1947) the fact that the

[1] It may be noted that in the experiment by Chapman and Volkmann quoted on the previous page, the group effect lost its power once the subjects had completed several trials. They then knew their own performance and regulated their level of aspiration according to their own score and not according to the (spurious) group score.

religion of the candidates for office in a new youth club was stated, produced new alignments among the voters. Jenness (1932) has a series of experiments in which subjects estimate the number of beans in a jar before and after discussing it with two other subjects. The groups are formed on the basis of the subjects' guesses before discussion. When the groups are such that one member is much above and the other much below the correct estimate, discussion enables all three members of the group to come to a correct conclusion, because of the tendency for individual scores to average out in the group. Where all three are above, or all three below, the correct estimate, they are merely confirmed in their first impression and no improvement in guessing occurs.

Group pressure, therefore, sometimes enables the individual to reach a correct solution, sometimes it confirms him in a wrong solution. It can even persuade him to move from one meaningless estimate to another. This is the conclusion to be drawn from Sherif's classical experiments in autokinetic perception phenomena. A tiny light shining in a completely dark room gives the subject no opportunity to relate the light to other objects in the room and so to judge its position correctly. Two or three subjects enter the room together and hear each other's guesses. Where it is impossible to judge in accordance with any frame of reference that the light has moved, the slightest allusion to this possibility is as a rule sufficient to produce the perception that it has done so. Even the extent to which it is perceived as having done so is entirely dependent on what quasi-information has been given by the guesses of others in the group. Even where the subjects did not previously know one another, they were influenced by each other. The subject is persuaded not only that a stationary light is moving, but even persuaded by social pressure to correct his estimate of the distance it moves and the direction in which it does so. The psychological reality of the group is unimportant here. Much more important is the fact that there was no information against which to evaluate the information provided by other members of the group.

The influence of the group may be even more marked than this. It may persuade a man to doubt the evidence of his own senses. The individual adjusts himself to the group not only by conscious conformity but also by inhibiting, sometimes consciously, sometimes unconsciously, his usual responses so as not to be far too removed from the average group response. The intensity of the pressure of the group, and the depth in the level of consciousness at which this pressure is experienced is perhaps best illustrated in an experiment by Asch (in Guetzkow, 1951). All but one of his subjects in a group were instructed to make deliberate mistakes in judging the relative lengths of bundles of sticks. The poor naive subject becomes more and more impressed by his inability to perceive what the others in the group see. In the end, he tends to make the same 'mistakes' as the others. There, are apparently, three types of psychological process underlying this behaviour. Some subjects really came to perceive the shorter sticks as longer. Others thought they must be subject to some kind of optical illusion which they sought to compensate for. Others again were sure that they were right and the other members of the group were wrong but they felt too diffident to persist in the face of such numbers. Similarly, Allport (1920) reports that estimates of weights are wider in range when individuals are tested in isolation than when they are in the company of others; smells from a bottle also are apparently never quite so disgusting or quite so exquisite when they are reported on in the group.

SUMMARY

(1) The individual conforms to the pressures imposed upon him.

(2) When in a group a man will orientate his actions with respect to others in the group.

(3) The physical presence of a group is not a necessary condition for conformity to its norms. The individual conforms in accordance with group pressure exerted on him in the past.

(4) In competition, the individual is most intensely aware of the presence of others.

(5) When there is no group whose norms are perceived as relevant in an unfamiliar situation, the norms of the culture will determine the behaviour of the individual.

Conversely, firm attachment to the norms of a group will enable a member to ignore or go against the norms of the culture.

(6) If success is valued, the opportunity to demonstrate one's skill acts as a stimulus to good performance.

(7) Under observation, the individual's performance will improve most in those aspects of the task which are most easily perceived by the observer.

(8) In situations of uncertainty, the information afforded by the group will be responsible for the individual's behaviour.

(9) The greater the uncertainty, the more the individual conforms to an estimate of the group average.

(10) The more information is available about the norms of the group, the more specific will be the individual's striving for success.

(11) The individual will tend to estimate success within the limits and of the kind approved by the group to which he seeks to conform.

(12) The striving for success may be qualified by the need to belong. The result is a levelling out of individual reactions: the range of deviations round the mean is narrowed.

CHAPTER SEVEN

The Evolution of Likes and Dislikes

THERE is a close relationship between group norms and the sentiments of group members toward one another. Basically, members who conform closely to the norms of the group are more popular than those who do not. This has been firmly established by Homans among others,[1] and there is no need to reproduce here the evidence on which this generalisation is based. It will, however, be worth our while to speculate a little on the genetic aspect of this relationship. The starting point of our argument comes from a study made by Thompson and Nishimura (1951, 1952). They presented their subjects with a list of one hundred personality traits and asked them to list their own personality, their ideal personality, a friend's personality and the personality of some acquaintance. They found high correlations between a subject's ideal personality and the personality he attributed to his friend, and between the ideal personalities of friends. For this reason they came to the conclusion that friendship is more frequently based on similarity of ideals than on similarity of personality traits. Thus individuals tend to choose

---

[1] The present chapter draws very largely on Homans, G. C., *The Human Group.* That great contribution to the study of small groups cannot be boiled down to one chapter nor would there be any point in recapitulating what has already been expounded so well. This chapter takes a good deal for granted. Its indebtedness to Homans' work must be apparent on every page.

It must be noted that norms are a kind of sentiment. That being so, a number of generalisations valid for friendship are also true for norms. Thus, for instance, just as further information about a group alters or confirms the norms of the members, so does further information about members alter or confirm the liking they have for one another. Similarly, the greater the amount of interaction between members, the more those processes will be accelerated, for interaction gives information. The more interaction, the more definite the norms, the more consensus about norms and the more consensus about the popularity ranking of the members. Similarity of norms induces increased interaction just as liking does. Many other examples may be found.

their friends because each seems to the other to reflect what he himself would like to be. This finding is, of course, easily confirmed by introspection. The ideal personality is the one you would like to be. Someone who is nearer to this ideal than you are is therefore likely to be liked. It is surely legitimate to generalise this argument to the small 5–6 member group. People with similar ideals like one another and are likely to choose the same kind of leader. All members evaluate one another in terms of an implied ideal personality for which all strive. The more a man fits into the ideal standards of the group the more popular he is likely to be, for he will represent the type of person all members would like to be.

This process of evaluation in terms of norms will patently cause some to be rejected for the same reasons that others are admired. Schachter (1951), for instance, took sociometric ratings in a group in which a discussion had taken place. Because of the discussion the members knew something of each other's viewpoint. Members who were perceived to hold views different from one's own were rejected, those who held the same views were rated highly on the sociometric scale. Conformity to a particular norm brings popularity from those who also subscribe to this norm.[1]

Interaction is a precondition for the growth of sentiments, whether of norms or of likes and dislikes. A man's emotional reaction to others is based on the way in which he perceives them. Social perception, just like perception of other objects, is determined in part by the characteristics of the object to be perceived and partly by the moods, expectations and needs of the perceiver. The more ambiguous the perceptual stimulus, the greater the importance of the subjective or functional elements in perception. The amount of information available to members about others in the group will therefore have an effect on the way in which they are perceived and on the feelings that are generated by them. Such information is often given by conversation, rightly regarded by commonsense as expressing the personality of the speaker. Therefore, the more interaction, verbal or other, takes place between the members of the group, the more information they will have at their disposal on which to base their likes and dislikes. And from this we may deduce that the greater the

[1] 'The fact that certain people are over-chosen or under-chosen implies that members share certain standards which the over-chosen exemplify and the under-chosen fall short of.' (Homans, 1954.)

amount of interaction the more definite the sentiments of group members toward one another.[1]

Let interaction continue over a period of time and let us assume that as interaction continues further information will be available to members of the group.

Having established on theoretical grounds that with continued interaction the sentiments of group members toward one another become more definite, we must now examine the empirical evidence at our disposal. Sentiment has as a rule been measured by the use of sociometric questionnaires, but these do not lend themselves easily to the proof of hypotheses in which interest is centred on the amount of sentiment in the group rather than on the popularity of particular members. The relative popularity of each member of a group may remain the same over a period of time; a sociometric questionnaire will not indicate that everyone is better liked now than at some previous time of testing if the ranking of members' popularity has remained the same. Bovard (1951) uses an eleven-point scale of liking on which each member evaluates every other member before and after a period of interaction. Such a scale is for our purposes an improvement on normal sociometric procedure because it measures the level of affect in a group in absolute rather than relative terms. In Bovard's study, the total number of points scored was significantly higher, i.e. had moved significantly to the *liking* extreme of the scale, after the period of interaction. Moreover, those groups in which more member-to-member interaction was observed had moved further to the liking extreme than had the groups which were characterised by more member-leader interaction. In the one case they talked freely to one another; in the other they tended all to talk to the same man, the leader. With a great deal of member-leader interaction, attention is focused less on other members than on the leader and thus less information is available to the group.[2] Therefore, it follows empirically as well as theoretically that the sentiments

---

[1] There may be circumstances in which this deduction is not valid. Information may produce doubt and confusion because seemingly contradictory personality-traits may emerge in the same person, but as there is no experimental work along these lines, we content ourselves with the warning that generalisations which follow are subject to this reservation.

[2] This detail will become very relevant to our discussion of leadership in Chapter 9.

in the leader-centred group are not so much affected by the period of interaction as is the case in the member-centred group.

The connection between interaction, norms and liking is also demonstrated by an unpublished study of the present writer's, of which a further account is given in the Appendix. In this study the development of relationships among group members who were initially strangers to one another was studied over a series of ten meetings. At the end of each meeting the members were asked to rank one another on a sociometric questionnaire. During the series of meetings the rankings which each member made came more and more to resemble the rankings made by the other members. This means that members of the group tend to agree more and more, in the course of ten meetings of the group, on the popularity status of each member. Moreover, in those groups in which interaction between members was more general, and in which each member spoke a good deal, this tendency toward consensus of opinion was more marked than in the more silent group in which there were marked differences in the interaction rates of members. We may therefore say that the more generally members participate in discussion, the greater the consensus of popularity in the group. This growing agreement is not specific to either likes or dislikes. If one takes separately the three highest or the three lowest popularity rankings in the group, the same trend is discernable. This is indeed a remarkable and unsuspected result in the circumstances, for these members had no opportunity to meet outside the experimental situation in order to gossip about the personality of their fellow members. Nor did they do so under observation. Yet agreement was arrived at. The word of the observer must be taken for the assertion that a content analysis would not reveal any direct indication of the way in which this consensus was reached. With Bales' (1950) analytic methods one might find that the increasingly popular members were increasingly shown approval, praise and support. It may be that when a slightly higher rate of receiving contributions of this kind becomes apparent to members that the tendency becomes accelerated. The observer can only repeat that this was in no way apparent to her.

THE STUDY OF GROUPS

Let there be differences in the communication rates of members.

If we recognise the relationship between information available about a man and his popularity in the group, we ought to find a relationship between volubility and popularity, with the more voluble members better liked than quieter members. In the course of the unpublished study referred to just above, the observer kept a record of the amount each member contributed to the conversation. It proved possible to show that the most voluble members were also the most popular and that members who spoke very little were regularly ranked lowest on the sociometric scale. This finding confirms that members of the group need some information before they can make up their minds as to whom they like. Where this information is not available, e.g. when a member does not communicate, the other members ignore him. At least at the beginning of a series of meetings of a new group, information of this kind is of the highest importance. It seems that anyone prepared to supply it is *ipso facto* better liked.

The relationship between popularity and volubility may well hold throughout the development of a group, but other factors than those stated above are likely to be involved. It may be suggested that a certain social control is exercised by members of a well-established group. When a group is fully developed it seems likely that members are more or less 'allowed' to speak and that the more popular members are less likely to be interrupted than the less popular. Some evidence for this view was suggested in a previous chapter.[1] It takes time, however, for a system of control to develop and most experimental groups are disbanded before such a stage could be reached. The more is the pity.

So far the evidence has led to the conclusion that an increase in interaction will lead to an increase in liking (see Homans, 1950). Common sense suggests that this cannot always be the case. Further information about a person may surely reveal traits which confirm a feeling of dislike just as clearly as they may reveal more favourably regarded traits. By investigating the circumstances in which the rule does not hold we may gain some theoretical advantage. There are, to a pessimist, no obvious reasons why one should come to like a

[1] See page 33.

94

man better when one gets to know him. George Homans is an optimist.

' "Friendliness" unquestionably conceals a complicated process. For one reason or another, you associate with someone for a period of time; you get used to him; your behaviour becomes adjusted to his, and his to yours; you feel at home with him and say he is a good fellow. The friendliness may be no more than the emotional reflection of adjustment and this is perhaps the reason that your liking for someone is so often independent of his personality. You can get to like some pretty queer customers if you go around with them long enough. Their queerness becomes irrelevant' (p. 115).

There are three ways in which the problem of interaction and dislike may be attacked. First, it is important to remember that many groups have no barriers to entrance or exit. In these circumstances, if a man feels that others do not like him, or if he does not like them, he will leave the group. Among those who remain, interaction may well lead to greater liking. Evidence that enforced interaction between those who are not prepared to like one another and would rather not interact does lead to hostility is given by Hughes (1946) among others. The situation is graphically summed up by Riecken and Homans (1954, p. 804).

'Hughes described the situation in one room of a plant where the members of three-man teams, who worked closely together in making a product, were nearly all Poles (as well as often being kin and neighbours). These teams were able to control the choice of new employees to be added to the teams. When management attempted to introduce individual Negroes into these teams, the Polish workers effectively forced them to quit by "a not very subtle, but very effective torture".'

Second, it may be that many dislikes spring from misunderstandings which further interaction may correct. Bovard justified this viewpoint in detail. According to him verbal interaction leads to a correction of distorted perception. One has an image of oneself. If others do not share this image, the individual will feel discomfort and will attempt to rectify it. If he is successful in his attempt and others 'understand him correctly' he will like them the better for it. An experience which had been painful is thus turned into one that gives pleasure.[1] Third, we may examine the circumstances in which the generalisation 'interaction leads to liking' does not hold. This is what we will proceed to do next.

ASSUMPTION THREE

Let interaction be frequent and of a kind which gives little information about the sentiments of others.

The possibility of misunderstandings between members of the group is a constant danger. Great care must therefore be exercised not to hinder the opportunities for correcting the impression gained of other members of the group. If members of the group behave autistically and cut themselves off from communication with others, mistaken impressions will persist and morale in the group will be low.

There are experimental situations in which only task-related or otherwise impersonal communication takes place and expressions of sentiment are inhibited, either by the instruction of the experimenter or by the attitudes of the group members. If no expressions of liking are allowed to take place (either verbal or behavioural, e.g. offering sweets) a sociometric test will show surprisingly few mutual choices. In the study more fully described in the Appendix, each of six group members had two sets of five choices to distribute each week. More often than not, none of these choices were returned. This misfitting persisted over ten weeks; the members never learned to choose those who chose them. The reason for this was implicit in the situation which made it impossible for them to gossip about each other or to see each other outside the experimental framework. The members of the group avoided discussing personalities in the experimental sessions and had no opportunity for those private meetings during which personal qualities are customarily discussed and assessed in normal life. As a rule, the experimental set-up compensates for the inhibition of the spontaneous development of mutual choices by making known the results of the sociometric questionnaire. Our members had no access to the completed questionnaire. There was no opportunity to come, even implicitly, to such agreements as 'You choose me and I'll choose you.' The observer kept the returns to the

---

[1] 'Oh sweet and lovely lady be good,
I am so awf'ly misunderstood,
Oh lady be good, to me.'

96

questionnaire confidential. Because she did not act upon the information obtained and thus reinforce the earlier tendencies by creating further opportunities for interaction, members' choices were not affected by the questionnaire results. The subjects could only use other evidence in making up their minds—what people said and to whom they said it. They could not be influenced by the desire to return the choices of those who had chosen them, or to cease choosing those who had rejected them. The evidence they obtain is sufficient to produce a popularity ranking shared by the members of the group; it is not sufficient to ensure mutuality of choice.

Not all interaction will give information about the personality of the speakers. There are many situations in which communication is restricted, in one way or another, so as to minimise the amount of personality-related information gained through interaction. George Homans has examined a number of such cases, where task performance is urgent, or where convention holds that communication must be strictly task-related, e.g. between foreman and worker, or between social classes. In such cases, he finds that sentiments are indeed more tinged with respect than affection. The external system ('those elements of group behaviour and their interrelationships in so far as they constitute a solution to the problem 'How shall the group survive?' Homans 1950, p. 90) may exercise such pressure on the group that there is no opportunity for any communication except of a strictly task-related kind.[1]

The amount of task-related information transmitted from member to member is only rarely in itself an indication of liking. Thus Homans: 'Persons who feel sentiments of liking for one another will express those sentiments in activities *over and above* the activities of the external system'. The amount of interaction in the internal system—the extent to which members interact in ways not required by the task—is likely to be both cause and effect of liking in the group and may in certain cases be a good index of the level of friendship in the group. The distinction between interaction in the external system and interaction in the internal system is such as to make the

---

[1] The concept of the external system is a very useful one. At its most general, it allows us to distinguish between those elements in a situation which shall be analysed in detail, and other elements which are noted only in their effect on the elements on which interest is focused. More particularly, the concept is used to distinguish interaction necessitated by the task from interaction connected with the sentiments of members. This will become a crucial distinction in the next chapter.

difference between them a measure of the level of sentiment in the group. It may well be more economical and convenient to measure sentiment in this way. Some very interesting relationships not covered by the sociometric test might come to light. There are, however, conditions, which we shall begin to discuss under the next assumption, in which such interaction is likely to be hostile rather than neutral.

ASSUMPTION FOUR

Let the pressure of the environment increase.

The concept of the pressure of the external system provides explanations for a number of theoretical problems. Let us first take a very extreme case. If interaction and liking vary directly, so that when one increases the other increases also, why, we may ask, does this process ever stop, why don't members go on liking each other better and better as they interact more and more? A simple answer would be that they are members of many groups and that they have to distribute their emotional energy between all the many people with whom they interact. There is a limit, one may assume, to the number of people one can love, and though this limit may differ for different people, it does exist. But let us aim at a self-denying ordinance and not explain social facts in terms of individual psychology unless we are driven to it.

A sociological explanation would have to take a different line. It has been stated that some interaction is necessary for the performance of the task. Sentiment also expresses itself in interaction, but it expresses itself more in interaction within the internal system. Whether or not a man has emotional limits, it is indisputable that within a given period of time only a limited amount of interaction can take place. If all the interaction occurs within the internal system, the task won't get done. If the task is not done, the group (as we have defined it, with an aim that partly defines the group) will disappear. The external system therefore imposes its limits on activity in the internal system and thus limits the growth of friendship. How soon this limit is reached depends on the amount of interaction that the task requires and on the urgency of the task, i.e. the amount of interaction in the external system necessary for survival within a given period of time.

Next we must remember that a group does not have absolute

98

control over its environment and the environment may at times exert such pressure on the group as to determine the type of task the group must deal with. When survival becomes an urgent problem, the energies of all members must be devoted to whatever task is necessary to survive. This means that interaction between members has to take place exclusively, or as nearly so as possible, in the task area, i.e. in the external system. Therefore, there will be a reduction in interaction in the internal system. There will be no interaction except that which is directly necessary for the performance of the task. A group fighting for its survival will often find that the members are more involved in the group as a result. But unless a special function of 'morale builder' evolves, sooner or later a point comes at which the effects mentioned earlier in this chapter tend to diminish. Friendship needs to be maintained through interaction, and task-related interaction is less likely to give information concerning the personalities of members. Norms and values are shared by friends; when there is less interaction there will be less uniformity of norms and less pressure to conform; the values of members or of cliques of members will diverge from one another. And if the group originally came together for reasons not directly related to the performance of tasks, if the commitment to and performance of tasks sprang initially out of a surplus of energy released by pleasure in one's fellow-members, the zest for task performance will decrease. Thus we get the condition sometimes called 'low morale'.

Now we shall find later that two forms of social control operate in the group, corresponding to the two forms of authority, deriving from function or from status, which we discussed in the earlier part of this book. One form of control is exercised through the knowledge that members have of each other's abilities and their respect for them; it is cemented by friendship and similarity of norms, which are in turn upheld by freedom of communication. The other form of control is restricted to certain members of the group, who manipulate others through rewards and who attain a leadership position for reasons other than expertise.

When survival becomes an urgent problem for the group, the system of control tends to change. Instead of control through the mutual liking of members, quite a different, less spontaneous, control comes about. Members are induced to obey other members by the reward that the latter have at their disposal. The more control of this kind is exercised, the less members like it and the less the controlling members are liked. This state of affairs is characteristic of highly centralised groups in which peripheral members have little opportunity for participating in the decision-making process. And indeed, by assuming that those who exercise control enjoy doing so, we may see that the more stable and centralised the group, the sooner a state of urgency will be perceived and the more power will be assumed by central members.[1]

ASSUMPTION FIVE

Let the task or the task structure be disliked.

When the environment is adverse, the group must try to bring about a more favourable condition. This task may not be one naturally congenial to the group members and it may necessitate a type of organisation which is also uncongenial. In such straits the natural inclinations of group members have to be ignored. But commitment to a cause is seldom so complete that no reluctance is felt when one's own desires and freedom of action have of necessity to be abandoned. The nearer the group comes to committing itself to an uncongenial task or to one the outcome of which is uncertain, the greater the dislike of the situation. It is therefore not surprising that Bales (1953, with Parsons and Shils) finds that 'the nearer a group comes to taking a decision and committing itself to a course of action, the more frequently the group's interaction will be of a social-emotional rather than a task-related kind'. This is presumably so because at that stage, freedom of action is coming to be restricted and this causes tensions which have to be resolved.

The group in which members have no more than neutral sentiments to one another is already in a dangerous and unstable state. When other circumstances are added, e.g. where the task is disliked or the setting in which it must be performed is disliked, the sentiments of the members will tend to be coloured by hostility to one another. The dislike must be projected on to something that will allow for expression. This may be either the product of the labour (i.e. the end result of the task) or it may be other members of the group.[2]

[1] This discussion is developed further on pages 137–139.
[2] This may help toward explaining the puzzling finding reported by Bovard (*op. cit.*) that members rate their liking for 'the group' higher than their average rating for all members. Presumably, they attribute the limitation on their freedom of action to control from others and they react by a reduction in their liking for others. They do not,

This is liable to happen even where some knowledge about the other members already exists. That is to say the dislike of the situation may be so intense as to depress the existing level of sentiment in the group.

Thibaut (1950) gives a case in which dislike of the situation actually depressed for certain members the existing level of friendliness in the group. He consistently favoured some boys at the expense of others in the group. The favoured few played what were generally regarded as the more exciting roles in various games, e.g. they threw the balls through hoops held by the less favoured boys. These boys all knew one another. At the beginning of the game they had as many friends in their own team as in the other. At the end of the games they chose more friends from within their own team than from the other team. Each team must have regarded the other as part of the disliked environment and rejected them for this reason. There is, however, one exception. There were some boys in the less favoured team who had not many friends either in their own or in the other team. They dissociated themselves from their own team and tended at the end of the games to prefer boys in the other team. It was the nature of the task that made them change their allegiance, and not a liking for the boys.

In the classic studies reported by Lippitt, Lewin and White—these are so well known that they need not be described in detail here—the *democratic* leader encouraged interaction between the boys, the *authoritarian* leader arranged the situation so that the boys were compelled to interact with him a good deal of the time. The interchange of information between the boys would therefore be greater in the former than in the latter group. Moreover, in the latter group the work was not chosen by the boys and it is therefore reasonable to assume that they were less involved in the task than were the boys in the democratically led group. The lack of information in the autocratically led group, and their consequent indifference to one another, together with their relative indifference to the task makes for an inflammable situation which might easily turn into a hostile one. This is, in fact, exactly what happens. Rapid changes in the composition of sub-groups are reported in the authoritarian group as members attempt to gain status at each other's expense; in the end, scape-goating is resorted to as the only way in which the necessary

however, recognise 'the group' as exercising control and therefore their liking for it is not depressed.

feeling of superiority can be gained. It will be remembered that the autocratically led groups also took no interest in or even expressed hostility toward the product of their labour. This is obviously another way in which the hostility, generated by the pressure of the system imposed on them, may show itself.

That it is the situation rather than the member who generates the dislike is also suggested by a further refinement in Kelley's study.[1] He introduced the possibility that members might be able to change their status half-way through the meeting. In half the high-status groups and half the low-status groups, he said he might have to change over some people from one task to another at half-time. One thus obtains four types of sub-groups: high-status mobile, and non-mobile; low-status mobile, and non-mobile. (This enabled him, incidentally, to ask at the end of the experiment which members wanted to change. By this means he was able to confirm that the low-status groups saw themselves as low, as these wanted to change their jobs more frequently than the others.) Mobility has an effect on the amount of irrelevant communication. Mobile low-status members who expressed a desire to move up had a significantly lower irrelevance score than non-mobile low-status members or than mobile low-status members who did not want to move up. The possibility of being moved to another group makes the low-status groups slightly more attractive to members, and the high-status groups correspondingly less attractive. This, one might say, stands to reason, but it is gratifying to see so human a situation reproduced in the laboratory. The non-mobile low-status members share some interesting characteristics with the high-status mobile group. They have by far the least number of cohesion and morale-building messages, they are more disruptive, they send fewer messages to other levels, i.e. they restrict communication voluntarily (group autisms) and chose fewer members of the other level in the final sociometric questionnaire. Kelley interprets this sort of behaviour in the one case as seeing other groups as threatening one's own good position and in the other to plain envy.

In a very different group studied by Back, escape took the form of neglecting the task for the performance of which they had met. This mechanism, made familiar by the study of industrial groups, shows itself when members do not derive sufficient satisfaction from

[1] See also page 33–34.

belonging to the group, which they therefore use as a stalking-horse to express their discontent with a situation from which they cannot escape. Back's (1948) study was of two discussion groups. In one group, A, the same members took up the largest amount of time at each session; in the other, B, different members tended to speak frequently according to mood and topic. Group A was observed to be significantly more emotionally toned and less work centred than group B, and its members were significantly more aggressive. That this is not due to personality difference is shown by the fact that, after training, conversation became more general in group A and as it did so, aggression diminished and devotion to the task increased. Communication here was not officially restricted, but it was restricted none the less and this evidently made the group less enjoyable and its members more restive.[1]

Thibaut's boys were favoured or deprived in playing congenial games; the boys in the experiments by Lippitt, Lewin and White were given, or deprived, of the opportunity to gain status; Kelley's groups were divided not only in that some were allotted high-status tasks and others not, but that some feared to lose their position and others hoped to gain it; Back's members were striving to make their voices heard. In all these cases, the members were in fact compelled to compete by the circumstances in which they found themselves. No wonder that their kind of behaviour markedly resembled that of a competitive group. In a competitive group some members have, or are more likely to obtain, what others want. In all situations where a sub-group has privileges which everyone wants, we can recognise the characteristics of the competitive group: restricted communication and hostility between members. It will be remembered that Deutsch (1949) found that in a co-operative group, members interact more and know more about one another than members of the competitive group. Their estimation of one another is also more realistic. Needless to say, they are also more friendly towards one another.[2]

ASSUMPTION SIX

Let us assume control by one member of the group.

If members do not like to have their freedom of action restricted by the impersonal force of circumstance, will not the situation be much aggravated when it is brought about by a member of the

[1] See also page 62. [2] See also page 34.

group? Where a man is perceived to be involving the group in actions uncongenial to it, his popularity is likely to suffer. This is likely to be so even when he controls the group in ways beneficial to it, 'for its own good'. Thus Bales reports that the 'highest participator', who tends to make more suggestions as to what shall be done than other members, is relatively little liked. He is seen as exercising control and will appear responsible for the resulting discomfort. We may therefore think that hostile reactions to control are not necessarily *generated* by high-status members, although the group will vent its resentment on them. The most 'directive' member will become the scapegoat. This situation is clearly outlined by Parsons, Bales and Shils (1953):

'We might tentatively advance the proposition that the traditional sociometric methods of determining 'leaders' are appropriate only to situations where there is no specific and well-defined instrumental task. As soon as such a task is introduced there arises a demand for the performance of the new roles which the task creates. Initially the best-liked man may perform these roles, but as time goes on, a dissociation takes place: either (1) someone else who can perform these new roles more successfully comes to the fore, or (2) the sociometric leader becomes a task leader and ceases to be best liked' (p. 157).

ASSUMPTION SEVEN

Let there be sub-groups with characteristic norms in the group.
Although a group may have come together for the performance of a task, the meaning of the task to its participants will inevitably be coloured by the differing value systems of its members. In this way, many smaller sub-groups may exist within the larger group, each of which subscribes to somewhat different values. This may involve friction between sub-groups over means to be employed or risks to be taken. Any frustrations met with in the pursuit of the task will tend to be channelled into hostility to other sub-groups and thus again scapegoating may develop.

In a group in which more than one norm has developed, the membership of each sub-group will tend to be determined by the importance which any one norm has for particular members. The norms which such a sub-group holds will thus be especially or even uniquely valued by those members. These norms will perform the function of distinguishing this sub-group from others. We have shown that conformity to a particular norm brings popularity from those others who also subscribe to this norm. Where there is more than one preferred norm in a group, there will be more than one popularity cluster. Such a process will work both ways. The existing mutually friendly members of a sub-group will tend to develop norms peculiar to that sub-group.[1]

When there is unity of norms in a group, sub-groups are less likely to form and all members are likely to agree on how much they like each other. Whenever sub-groups have had the opportunity to evolve norms of their own, discrepancies in the popularity rankings are likely to occur, for the different sub-groups will value different characteristics and therefore they will differ in the criteria by which they rank one another. There may then be a struggle for the norms of one sub-group to become supreme and recognised by the others and this will show itself in a struggle for status between two or more high-status members from the different sub-groups. Heinecke and Bales (1953) studied groups of two kinds. In one type of group, members agreed more or less where everyone stood in the status-hierarchy. In the other type there was no such initial agreement. The first few meetings became a battlefield in which the members fought between themselves for dominance, but the period of this clash was shorter in the groups in which there was initially some consensus about the status-hierarchy. In these groups, the struggle was also more or less confined to initially high-status members. After this battle, they apparently come to some agreement. Honour is satisfied and the high-status members retire into the background and let the lieutenants take over overt control, they themselves controlling the lieutenants. This kind of group was more satisfied with its solutions to the problem than were the groups where agreement on the status of members was not reached. They are also more efficient in the sense that impartial observers thought their solutions were better.

---

[1] This can only come about in a group if there is a certain amount of privacy. The process outlined above, in which sentiment clusters and norms emerge simultaneously, could not occur in groups whose members, whatever their potentially common interests, and therefore norms, and therefore mutual affinities, have to meet only on occasions on which all other members are present too. Too many interruptions and disturbances from members belonging to potentially different sub-groups would occur for kindred spirits to be able to identify one another. In other words, the members must also be able to interact more within their sub-groups than with other sub-groups.

Heinecke and Bales suggest that once the problem of status is settled, time can more easily be given to the task and people enjoy themselves because there is less bickering and less overt control.

SUMMARY

(1) The greater the amount of interaction between members
  (a) the more information is available about the personality of members.
  (b) the more definite the sentiments of members toward each other;
  (c) the more consensus concerning the popularity status.

(2) Norms are sentiments. The generalisations valid for sentiments are valid for norms.

(3) Interaction corrects errors of judgement concerning the personality of other group members.

(4) The more interaction, the more positive is the sentiment towards others in the group and towards those who interact frequently in particular, except:
  (a) where interaction does not give information about personalities;
  (b) where the task is disliked;
  (c) where interaction does not give information about the sentiments of other members;
  (d) in two other cases which will be discussed fully in Chapter Nine:
    (i) where control is attempted by a member with deviating norms;
    (ii) where sub-groups have different norms.

(5) Friendship is more frequently based on similarity of ideals than on similarity of personality.

(6) The difference between interaction in the internal and interaction in the external system is a measure of the level of sentiment in the group.

(7) Members who attempt to control the group tend to lose their popularity.

(8) Where interaction is frequent and information about personality low, there tend to be few mutual friendships.

(9) As the pressure of the environment increases:
    (i) interaction in the internal system decreases,
    (ii) division of labour and restricted communication increase.
This may cause friendships to decrease.

(10) Deviance from the norms of the group results in decreased liking.

(11) The following factors tend to strengthen one another:
    A likes B and B likes A;
    A knows B likes him and vice versa;
    A interacts with B;
    A and B share ideals;
    A and B interact more with one another than with other members of the group.

CHAPTER EIGHT

Sentiment in the Group: The Expressive Dimension

THE four chapters which now follow attempt to place the material so far presented within a larger theoretical framework. In this attempt we lean heavily on the work of R. F. Bales, and somewhat more lightly on that of Talcott Parsons. The reader's attention is requested to rest not so much on the fact that some of the ideas of these sociologists will be criticised and modified, but rather on the fact that it is now possible to progress in the theory of small groups by using and building on the efforts of other workers. The trend of the theory is becoming more clearly defined; a large and consistent body of fact and theory, acquired from many different sources and interests, is developing. This is a matter for rejoicing.

Bales' contribution is second to none. It is fruitful for two reasons. First, it gives us a scheme for the event-by-event observation of the group processes from which larger categories may be built up and thus makes possible the verification of hypotheses at the level of the group's interaction pattern. Second, it allows for the construction of theories of more general sociological interest by stating explicitly the relationships between the categories. Indeed, each category can be defined in terms of its relationship to other larger classes and to other categories at its own level; that is to say, a category is defined not by its content, but by its position in a more general system of action. As the position of one planet may be inferred from the relationships known to exist between the other planets, so the existence of a particular interaction process, at a specified point in time or in a sequence, can be inferred from what we know of the other processes that have been observed in the group.

Bales' observation scheme enables the observer to identify each act under one of the following six headings: communication (categories 6 and 7), evaluation (categories 5 and 8), control (categories 4 and 9), decision (categories 3 and 10), tension reduction (categories 2 and 11) and reintegration (categories 1 and 12). Each of these headings is split into positive and negative. Thus a *positive* act of communication is to *give information*, a *negative* act to *ask for it*. The complete schedule is reproduced below.

The system of categories used in observation and their major relations.

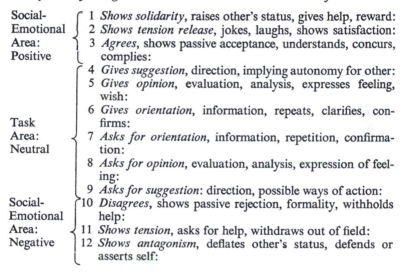

Social-Emotional Area: Positive
- 1 *Shows solidarity*, raises other's status, gives help, reward:
- 2 *Shows tension release*, jokes, laughs, shows satisfaction:
- 3 *Agrees*, shows passive acceptance, understands, concurs, complies:

Task Area: Neutral
- 4 *Gives suggestion*, direction, implying autonomy for other:
- 5 *Gives opinion*, evaluation, analysis, expresses feeling, wish:
- 6 *Gives orientation*, information, repeats, clarifies, confirms:
- 7 *Asks for orientation*, information, repetition, confirmation:
- 8 *Asks for opinion*, evaluation, analysis, expression of feeling:
- 9 *Asks for suggestion*: direction, possible ways of action:

Social-Emotional Area: Negative
- 10 *Disagrees*, shows passive rejection, formality, withholds help:
- 11 *Shows tension*, asks for help, withdraws out of field:
- 12 *Shows antagonism*, deflates other's status, defends or asserts self:

The development of Bales' ideas can be studied by a comparison between his earlier *Interaction Process Analysis*, from which the above scheme is taken, and the later *Working Papers in the Theory of Action*, in which he collaborated with Parsons and Shils. We shall not describe these here in detail, since we shall diverge from both.

In *Interaction Process Analysis* Bales had already tentatively discussed the connection between his twelve observation categories and three larger ones, which roughly corresponded to the old psychological distinction between conation, cognition and affect. At that time Bales concluded that no direct relationship existed. In the *Working Papers* the issue is a little blurred, but it is likely that he changed his mind, for there we find a table in which such an attempt is made. The relevant aspects of the table are reproduced here.

109

Bales' categories	Larger categories
Reintegration	Integrative Dimension
Tension reduction ⎫	Expressive Dimension
Decision ⎭	
Control	Instrumental Dimension
Evaluation ⎫	Adaptive Dimension
Communication ⎭	

Expressive, instrumental and adaptive are taken to correspond roughly to affective, conative and cognitive respectively. In order to pursue our argument in the way we want to, we shall use a rather different scheme.

Because we have been considering sentiment in the two previous chapters we shall start our discussion with the expressive dimension, the 'social-emotional' areas of the group process. Expressive behaviour for us, however, will include both the categories of reintegration and of tension reduction. The categories of decision and control are discussed in the next chapter and those of evaluation and communication in the one after. Integration is a different kind of concept altogether which we shall discuss in Chapter Eleven.

The first of the alterations we shall make to the schemes outlined above is to boil down, purify, and—to continue our kitchen metaphor—clarify the categories of reintegration and tension reduction. We shall reduce it to one observation category, that of expressive behaviour.[1]

There are sentiments in the group. We cannot see them; we have to infer them from the interaction process. What we can see is the expression of friendliness and hostility; underlying these expressions we assume their existence; underlying their existence we assume a frame of reference composed of values—a system of standards which determines the sentiments of people toward one another. Expressive behaviour is taken to be the manifestation of underlying sentiment, both at the level of sentiment toward persons, and at the deeper level of sentiment toward values, which is a part of that total frame of reference which leads a man to prefer one man or one action to another in a given set of circumstances.

The total frame of reference includes, of course, knowledge and

[1] One reason for doing so is that the two categories are not very easily distinguishable; another that the positive and negative do not seem to be truly symmetrical, i.e. the opposite of asking for help (showing tension) is not really to laugh or to joke, but rather to give help, which is subsumed by Bales under 'showing solidarity'.

information as well as values, aims, goals, or standards, but that aspect of the frame of reference is most clearly manifested by inter-action in the adaptive dimension which we shall discuss in Chapter Nine. The combination of these two aspects of the frame of reference is manifested when a decision has to be made in which knowledge is used for the fulfilment of a value; this is discussed in Chapter Ten.

In the adaptive dimension and in decision-making, the require-ments of the task determine the interaction pattern of the members: in the former dimension free communication is most efficient, in the latter, it is sometimes free communication and sometimes a rather centralised organisation of the group. This makes it more difficult to infer from interaction what the sentiments of members are. It is only when members are not compelled by the task to interact in the most efficient way for the performance of the task, that inferences con-cerning the feelings of members are not confused by task-related interaction patterns which are to some extent superimposed on the sentiment structure of the group. Interaction in the task-related areas is laid down by the nature of the task and by the necessities of the situation in which the group finds itself, in short, by the external system.[1] Interaction in the expressive dimension is interaction in the internal system; it is created by the group's elaboration of the inter-action pattern laid down by the external system and consists of interaction *over and above* that required by the task.

'We shall not go far wrong if, for the moment, we think of the external system as group behaviour that enables the group to survive in its environment and think of the internal system as group behaviour that is an expression of the sentiments toward one another developed by the members of the group in the course of their life together.' (Homans, 1950, pp. 109–110.)

The criterion by which expressive behaviour is recognised is there-fore twofold: expression of feeling and irrelevance to the task. All interaction that does not immediately concern the task, that is not concerned with the transmission of relevant information or with proposals as to what shall be done about the task, we shall call expressive behaviour.

[1] The correspondence of Bales' social-emotional area to Homans' internal system was suggested to me by a postgraduate student, Mrs. June Norris, to whom I am very grateful.

111

EXPRESSIVE BEHAVIOUR

(a) positive. Main criteria—irrelevance, friendliness.

The positive end of the expressive category is recognised by inter-action in Bales' categories 1 and 2 (i.e. reintegration and tension reduction) as described in the appendix to *Interaction Process Analysis*. The main stress there, however, is laid on the expression of liking for persons. We include also manifestations of liking for the kind of task: 'We're doing fine, isn't this fun, this is really well worth doing', etc., and of liking to be in the group: 'it's pleasant to be here; I'm having a lovely time; I'm glad I managed to come', etc.

(b) negative. Main criteria—irrelevance, hostility.

Again, Bales' description in the categories 11 and 12 (i.e. tension expression, reintegration) provide a useful guide, but we differ from Bales in that we include only such interaction as is irrelevant, i.e. does not help or hinder progress toward the task. Interaction that is expressive of dislike for a proposal to act in a certain way we rele-gate to the category of (dis) agreement which is discussed in Chapter Ten.[1] On the other hand, some of the behaviour categories by Bales in the category of (dis) agreement (category 10), is included here.

'Any situation in which an emotional response would be ex-pected, where the actor refuses to give applause, or is unappreci-ative, unacknowledging, ungrateful, unallured, "hard to please", "hard to get", is included. Includes passive forms of rejection, such as remaining immobile, rigid, restrained, silent, close-mouthed, uncommunicative, inexpressive, impassive, imperturb-able, reticent, responseless, in the face of overtures of the other. Includes any passive withholding of love or friendship, any indi-cation that the actor is psychically insulted, detached, isolated, indifferent, disinterested, impersonal, aloof, formal, distant, un-social, reserved, secluded, unapproachable, exclusive, or forbid-ding. Refraining from intimacies and confidences where the other appears to be seeking this kind of response is included. All un-determined member-to-member contacts, that is, asides, whisper-ing, winks, etc., while the main discussion is going on between others are classified in this category as rejections by both parti-

---

[1] The following distinction must be noted. If a member proposes that the group shall rehearse a play and another says that he hates play-acting, that is a task-related con-tribution. If the group decides to act a play and during a rehearsal a man says he hates play-acting, that is expressive behaviour.

112

cipants of the rest of the group. Working at something other than the problem with which the group is concerned, when there is an expectation that all will be attending or actively participating is included. Speaking or paying attention to outsiders, such as observers, when the group as a whole is working on another problem is included.'

Generally the behaviour is the opposite of that subsumed under positive, that is to say, expressing directly or indirectly a *dis*like of the members, the group or the nature of the task.[1]

REWARDS

It is clear that liking members and the nature of the task or the group is an inducement to stay in the group and that disliking the members and the nature of the task or the group is a disincentive. As a rule, membership of a group is a mixed blessing. There are advantages and disadvantages. In deciding whether he shall stay in the group a member will weigh up the balance of advantages and disadvantages, the amount that he is given and the amount that he must give.[2] Members contribute something to the group and receive something from it; there will be a point at which membership becomes worth while and another at which it will cease to be so. This 'economist's' way of looking at group behaviour, in terms of incentives and disincentives, is very useful. It is suggested by Simon (1952). We will, however, complicate his model a little by comparing the balance of rewards that one group has to offer with that of other groups whose membership is open to the aspirant. A group that wants to keep its members must provide them with a sufficient inducement to make them deaf to the lure of other groups.

Now some members may have more attractive alternative choices open to them than others have. They will therefore need a greater inducement to stay in the group. Similarly, there may be more and

---

[1] Neutral irrelevances, e.g. 'let's go to the pictures' must be scored positively when the main sense is an expression of friendliness, and negatively when the main sense is in fact 'I don't like what we are doing at present'.

[2] We may distinguish between rewards which are distributive—if one man is given more another member must necessarily be given less, as is the case with money or status, and rewards which are free—so that the satisfaction of one member is independent of and may even promote the satisfaction of another, as is the case with friendship. The achievement of aims, which must be considered as a reward, is an interesting special case. In the co-operative group, achievement belongs to the latter and in the competitive group to the former category.

I   113

less indispensable members. In this case, inducements must be related to the degree to which the working of the group would be impaired if a member were to leave, even if he does not wish to leave permanently (as in strikes or lock-outs). The same argument is valid, though necessarily more complicated, if we hold, unlike Simon, that there are degrees of group membership, if, that is to say, there are degrees of the extent to which a member may participate in the group and devote himself to its interest. For a relatively small 'contribution' of this kind, a member may not expect much reward. But even here the notion of indispensability is important.

Logically Simon is plainly right when he assumes a point at which the satisfaction of remaining in the group outweighs by the smallest conceivable margin the advantages derivable from non-membership. Practically speaking, however, this must be a highly unstable position and one which in actual fact rarely corresponds to the balance of advantages which members obtain from the group. For when one group is only one of many sources of satisfaction to a group member, the slightest change in the inducements other groups are able to offer would persuade the member to change his allegiance. Thus it will be remembered that in Thibaut's experiment some members changed their group allegiance when they realised that other groups performed tasks more attractive than their own.[1] Unless we assume that a group can control other rival groups, the group will have to allow its members a larger than minimum amount of satisfaction, so that it may have some room for adjustment if other groups change their systems of rewards.

What are the satisfactions with which a group supplies the members and what are the disadvantages of group membership? Let us sum up what we have learned in the two preceding chapters.

Rewards spring, with the exception of financial reward, from the shared value system which we assume to be underlying positive expressive interaction in the group. More concretely, they may be summed up in the phrase 'the pleasures of being sure that others will respond in the desired way'. Friendship is therefore one of the group products from which the individual profits. Friends are willing, even happy, to respond to one another in the way that is desired of them, to do what they ask of each other, sometimes at the expense of wishes that they would otherwise have gratified. Friendship is ex-

[1] See page 101.

pressed *par excellence*, not in the co-operative performance of a task, but in interaction over and above that required by the task. When the task is finished, the group does not break up. The task itself is not the *raison d'être* of the group. From the material introduced in this and the previous chapters, it will be clear that friendship is brought about and maintained to a very large extent through interaction in the positive category of social-emotional, expressive, behaviour.

Second, a shared frame of reference, both for values and for knowledge, makes interaction easier. It could hardly be otherwise. The members use a common idiom. They need not indulge in lengthy explanations or justifications of basic principles; they can take those for granted. People with very different norms find it hard to understand what the other is trying to say, harder to appreciate why he is saying it and very hard indeed to approve of it. Listeners to a radio discussion between Bertrand Russell and a Jesuit will appreciate how true this is. A shared frame of reference makes task performance easier, and that is rewarding in itself, but there is also a kind of reward in the very fact of using a common language. For this reason we get Air Force slang, nicknames, Greek tags, Cockney rhyming slang.

Third, a shared value system enables members to evaluate the different aims to which the group might devote itself in an order of preference. If a man joins a group because he finds the group's aims attractive, this means that in co-operating with them on a task he achieves an end valued both by him and by the others. The achievement of an end will be sufficient reward to keep him in the group.

Clearly all these factors have a cohesive function: members will be anxious to stay in the group because they value the tasks the group chooses to perform, because they like each other, because the common idiom strengthens in-group feeling and draws boundaries between in-group and out-group. A further impetus toward cohesion comes about because the three factors interact. Friendship brings with it an increased susceptibility to the norms of others, and people like one another because they share certain norms. They have an ideal personality in mind, something they strive for and by which they measure their own and other people's performance. If two people with similar standards meet, they will like one another, for they are striving after the same ends. Members of friendship groups

115

thus reinforce one another's ideals. If a man joins a group for friendship's sake, he becomes susceptible to the group's norms for friendship's sake and works co-operatively toward the group's goal because both he and they value it. Friendship and the achievement of an end will be sufficient reward to keep him in the group.

A man may join a group solely in order to carry out a task which he has not the skill or endurance to carry out alone. He teams up with other men. If he is fortunate, he will in the course of interaction begin to like them, begin to share their norms and to feel as unconstraining the pressure of control that membership brings in its wake. To expand the sequence already outlined: a man interacts with others in the performance of a task, begins to like them and becomes susceptible to their norms.

There are, however, finally, tasks for the efficient performance of which groups need to be of a certain size, or the group may need members of a certain kind, experts, for example. Gilchrist (1952) demonstrated that members may put the need to choose recruits who have demonstrated their ability above their desire to choose those they like or know. But this works both ways. Higher inducements have to be held out to such recruits than to those who are willing to join but have no special skill. Thus members may have to be recruited from those who are interested in rewards other than the achievement of a common aim or the friendship of members. Then a distribution of material reward has to be established to induce such persons to enter the group and to keep them there. In groups where friendship is not very close or norms are not greatly shared, difficulties of control and reward are likely to become important. It is interesting to realise that paid members who need to be rewarded financially and cannot be induced to work solely because they value the end to be achieved, tend to have less prestige than other members of the group. (Viz. Sherpas, Professionals, etc.)[1]

This enumeration of the group's rewards corresponds to the analysis of the kind of behaviour that is irrelevant to the task and expressive of friendliness in the group. Now let us look at disincentives.

The disadvantages of group membership are also manifold. First, freedom of action is restricted; one is subject to the decisions of other members; other members have a right to a certain amount of con-

[1] For this suggestion I am indebted to my former colleague, G. Duncan Mitchell.

116

sideration and may have to be cajoled and kept sweet to induce them to co-operate. The member has to give time and effort; demands may be made on him at inconvenient moments. Second, there may be disadvantages to belonging to a particular group, a group that does not give the member the appreciation to which he feels entitled or does not give him sufficient scope or recognition for his talents, whose members may irritate him, and other such discomforts.

In discussing disincentives we must also consider certain effects of the division of labour. Some of the disadvantages of such organisation have been discussed in Chapter Five. It is a disincentive to have to perform routine tasks at a lower level of responsibility than one's ability entitles one to; there is the danger of boredom and of overwork, and so on. Two other considerations must now be sketched in.

There are structures peculiarly suitable for the performance of certain kinds of tasks. These structures necessitate more interaction with some members, and less with others. Suppose a division of labour makes it necessary for a recruit to interact largely with those he likes less well, the ones whose previous level of interaction with him he felt to be quite appropriate. If that level of interaction was due to his ignorance of their good qualities, he may now come to like them better. If, however, it was due to the fact that he knew them and yet did not like them, he will now be unhappy. At the same time the task may necessitate his cutting down his interactions with those he did like and for the sake of whose company he may initially have joined the group. This will increase his dissatisfaction.

Moreover, a division of labour requires the control of some members by others. Although we cannot fully discuss the circumstances in which control is resented until Chapter Ten, we must mention that this may be so and that this will then operate as a disincentive.

If a man is emotionally involved in the task and anxious to see it accomplished, such effects may not be serious. He will content himself with the thought that this state of affairs will not last for ever. But if he only performs the task for the sake of his friends, he will be discontented, and he will either put pressure on the group to discontinue the task (and seek to be in a position where his pressure counts) or he will become discouraged and leave. This is a very unstable situation. If he does not like the group and they need him more than he needs them, they have to reward him in order to induce him to stay in the group. He will need additional inducements in the form of material rewards to compensate him for the control to which he is now subject, or in the form of status and control to compensate him for lending his skill to a group he does not care about.

Any distribution of rewards has to take into account that some members are more indispensable than others. Indispensable members have to be rewarded more highly than others, since their loss would be more serious. Lack of material reward is obviously a disincentive. Only slightly less obviously, great differences in rewards are a disincentive. One cannot indefinitely increase the rewards of some members even when it is not directly at the expense of others— as the disputes on differentials in wages may show. Morale is lowered when differences in reward are too great.[1]

That hostility results from such disincentives and that the unrewarding conditions described above have a disruptive effect is clear from the evidence produced in the previous chapter. It need not be recapitulated here.[2]

To sum up, then, the schematic representation of interaction in the expressive dimension is as follows:

> *positive* when indicative of satisfaction, when rewarding, when cohesive.

social-emotional behaviour,
interaction in the internal system,
irrelevance to task.

> *negative* when indicative of dissatisfaction, when unrewarding, when disruptive.

[1] See Bales (1950), pages 153 ff.

[2] It is important to realise that expressive behaviour *is not* an inducement; inducements are either material or spring from a shared frame of reference. They are only expressed in behaviour. The distinction is important and amusing. Quite often in theory there is a confusion between tension expression and tension reduction, and not infrequently in practice people want a show of appreciation more than they want affection. It is sometimes obliquely suggested that a 'tension reducer', someone who makes jokes and praises others when tension rises to make other members happy, is the solution to problems of dissatisfaction in the group. In the author's opinion the tension reducer is a pain in the neck. Unless his behaviour has an effect on the structure of the group, he serves no useful function. If there is tension in the group, a fault in the structure is responsible and only a structural alteration, one which redistributes obligations or rewards or changes the frame of reference of some members, will lower tension successfully and permanently. Tension reduction is a concept of a higher order; we shall discuss in Chapter 11. Here we are discussing the expression of feeling, good or bad.

The feeling of the group is manifested by expressive behaviour. From it, we may infer the sentiments of members towards one another, for instance, by the ratio:

$$\frac{\text{friendly irrelevant behaviour}}{\text{hostile irrelevant and task related behaviour (i.e. all other)}}$$

We have, moreover, assumed that behind the feelings of members toward one another lies a frame of reference. To the extent that it is shared, members will like one another. Chapter Ten will expand on this assumption.

We have also shown that a shared value system is rewarding in a number of ways and that rewards may be endangered by certain types of organisation.

Finally we have asserted that rewards have a cohesive function, disincentives a disruptive one.

Rewards are either material or, like friendship or a shared task, they may spring from a shared frame of reference.

This argument enables us to construct certain formulae.

$E+$ is the total positive expressive behaviour given in the group.

$E-$ is the total negative expressive behaviour given in the group.

$\bar{E}+$ and $\bar{E}-$ represent expressive behaviour received in the group.

The equivalents for a single member are $e+$, $e-$, $\bar{e}+$, $\bar{e}-$, respectively.

A popular member will be recognised by the large number of positive contributions he receives compared to the number of negative contributions he receives, but this must be considered in relation to the total expressive behaviour in the group.

Popularity of the ith member:

$$\frac{(\bar{e}+_i)}{(\bar{e}+_i) + (\bar{e}-_i)} \times \frac{E-}{E+} \times 100$$

A friendly man will be recognised by the proportion of positive contributions he makes out of his total expressive behaviour, but this must be considered in relation to the total expressive behaviour received in the group.

Friendliness of the ith member:

$$\frac{(e+_i)}{(e+_i) + (e-_i)} \times \frac{\bar{E}-}{\bar{E}+} \times 100$$

119

A man important in the cohesive dimension must be a man who is both popular himself and friendly with all other members. Obviously popularity and friendliness have to be combined in some way to indicate this role.

CHAPTER NINE

Communication as Adaptive Behaviour

A GROUP has to make continual adjustments to the environment if it is to survive. When the environment changes, the group has to change also and such changes have themselves to be regulated by further changes in the environment. Adaptation does for the group what cognition does for the individual. It entails the acquisition, storage and combination of the resources of information on which the group may draw when it considers the problem of its survival. It consists of the two observation categories of communication and evaluation. By communication we mean the transmission of information, just as Bales does. Bales has distinguished between communication and evaluation, but this is not necessary for the present purpose. In evaluation a communication is placed in a setting, either the setting of members' goals or the setting which relates a previous communication to other pieces of information. Basically, it is just a special type of information. Since we build up adaptation from communication and evaluation, we shall when we talk of these two categories together, call them A.

A good deal has necessarily already been said on the subject of the adaptive phase. All that has been said on the transmission of information[1] becomes relevant again. Although the next chapter will show that restricted communication in certain circumstances may speed up the decision-making process, free communication is essential for good adaptation. If a group is to adapt speedily, it must have a communication structure which allows the most rapid transmission of information.

Let us sum up briefly. All the consequences that may conceivably be relevant to the change which the group faces if it is to avert the danger to its survival must be brought into the open, and their like-

---

[1] See pages 40–75.

lihood and relative priority evaluated. The more information is available and the more freely it travels in the group, the better the task can be performed. The more links there are between members, the shorter the diameter is likely to be and the more efficient the spread of information. Moreover, the more links there are, the less likely the group is to suffer from the consequences of differentiation between members. Such freedom of interaction also corrects distortions in judgement and aids the correction of errors in the group.

We have seen in how many ways free communication in the group is threatened. When, for instance, the pressure of the environment is suddenly so great that the problem of survival becomes most urgent, there may not be an opportunity to canvass opinion in this free way. We have seen how consciousness of status operates against free communication. The lower-status members speak less and tend to make fewer suggestions; they influence the action process passively, by approval and disapproval rather than by positive advocacy of a policy. Peripheral or lower-status members are less likely to learn. They tend to sit back and let the central members do their thinking for them. (This is what made it so difficult for the highly organised star group to adjust to changing conditions when the pure colour marbles were exchanged for cloudy ones.)[1]

Not only differences in status but any kind of routinisation which influences members to delay in communicating information will have a bad effect. We know that groups with a leader show less equal participation than groups without a leader. The less differentiation between members therefore the better, but if differentiation is necessary or inevitable, it is important to stick to a routine, for peripheral members have been trained not to use their initiative. Where the organisation of the group is rigid, changes in the routine of the group endanger its survival. Lastly, when there are sub-groups loosely connected with the main group, the spread of information in the network is delayed. In fact, the less differentiation in the group the better. If there are leaders in the group they must see to it that they are sure that they are followed by the members. They must ensure some kind of feedback. But totally connected networks, without leadership, are the ideal at this stage.

We shall single out two group roles which are likely to be par-

[1] See page 69.

122

ticularly useful in the adaptive phase: direct access to the resources of information and indirect access to the same.

DIRECT ACCESS: THE OPEN CELL AND THE EXPERT

Because the group has to adjust to changes in the environment it is important to have adequate information concerning it and liaison with it. The group needs open cells for this purpose. These bring information from outside to the group, so that members may be well informed about the demands of the environment (and also about the techniques current in other groups which might usefully be adopted). Homans points out that often leaders are in the best position to know what is happening outside the group; they are in contact with leaders of other groups by virtue of their recognised position; they may be leaders just because they are the only ones that can give information about the environment.

Another type of open cell is the expert, the man who has a skill, usually acquired elsewhere, which he puts at the disposal of the group. For instance, a lecturer is assumed to have certain kinds of information which he must impart to the student in order that the student may achieve his goal and remain a member of his group. Another example may be drawn from the larger organisation. Sometimes there are members who have been allotted the special function of finding out about the environment, like the research section of an industrial firm. Their problem, like that of the lecturer, is often not one of being heard but of being understood or obeyed. What they think to be important may not be appreciated by the rest of the group. The problem of understanding and accepting information belongs to the next chapter; it depends not only on the existence of efficient communication channels, but also on the norms of the giver and of the recipient of the information. Where members do not share norms they may fail to appreciate the importance of a communication. If we assume, as we do here, that this difficulty does not arise, the problem is reduced to that of the efficiency of group networks. All that then needs to be added is that the open cell must be in a position to know whether he has been sufficiently well understood: there must therefore be a feedback from members to the information giver. There must be interaction: communication must not be a one-way process.[1]

[1] See the experiment by Heise and Miller outlined on page 66. We shall see later in the chapter that such feedback may bring a valuable sense of participation.

Even when the open cell is not one which is particularly related to an important part of the environment, and could not correctly be called an expert, the group gains much from easy interaction with the environment. A group may become too cohesive, so cohesive that it becomes incapable of adjusting to the environment. For in such a group there is a great uniformity of norms. Everyone has the same frame of reference, and these determine to a serious extent the group's expectations about what is going to happen next. They therefore routinise the behaviour of members toward one another and toward the environment. The establishment of such a routine is not necessarily a good thing for the group, although it saves effort and planning. The greater the routine of the group the more the ability to change tends to disappear. Routine behaviour of members toward the environment includes not only what is to be done to the environment (the task) but also the interpretation of the effect the environment is having on the group, i.e. the feedback from environment to the group. Part of such evaluations are, for instance, implied judgements about what is the most pressing problem that the environment is presenting to the group at a particular moment. If the group is one in which members have spent much of their time and have therefore been relatively isolated from other groups, not many new ideas will be forthcoming about the way the group should adapt to the changing environment, even though there may be complete agreement about what is to be done. Paradoxically, a new recruit, although he may imperil the equilibrium of the group,[1] may also may also bring the group such information as they need in order to survive.

All such open cells and experts are in the position of having direct access to resources. Bales suggests that they may be recognised by the number of questions a particular member is asked in the categories of communication, evaluation *and control* as compared to the total number asked by all members. Bales includes the asking for suggestions (the category of control). In our view (and perhaps in his later view) this cuts across the distinction of adaptation and goal achievement that we are anxious to preserve. It does not seem to involve any great theoretical wrench to change the concept of direct access to resources in such a way that the formula for any member i

---

[1] See page 152.

should read $\dfrac{(\bar{a} - _i)}{A -}$ × 100. 'A' stands for the problem of adaptation

in the group, a for that of the individual, the minus sign shows that we are concerned with the negative aspect of adaptation, i.e. asking questions rather than giving answers, the bar over a indicates questions received as distinct from questions asked. In words, the direct access to resources of the ith member is indicated by the number of questions of communication and evaluation asked by the group, expressed as a percentage of those asked of the ith member.

INDIRECT ACCESS TO RESOURCES

Restraints on free communication in the adaptive phase are ineffective and inefficient, that is to say, they make the process of communication and therefore of problem solving more difficult and they make it less enjoyable.

Hare (1952) studied groups of five and of twelve boys who discussed what was the best list of things to take camping. It will be remembered that the boys who were in the larger group were dissatisfied with the outcome of the discussion. One reason for this has already been stated: they felt they had not been given a sufficient chance to put their own views. We may now suggest a second reason. Larger groups need some organisation to give everyone a fair chance to contribute without getting in the way of someone else. They need someone to draw them out. In Hare's groups, the discussion leader was himself one of the boys, appointed, not elected, because he was a good Boy Scout, and thus an 'expert'. But he was young and inexperienced and he had not the skill, so necessary in larger groups, to organise the members so as to avoid confusion. Only a half-hearted allegiance was accorded to whatever plan finally emerged from this collection of members all too inhibited to say what they preferred. The encouragement of definite proposals is therefore an important function performed in the group.

Some confirmation of this supposition is provided by Hemphill (1950). Hemphill asked subjects to describe the groups to which they belonged. His findings show that in the larger groups the leader was expected to do a number of things which in the smaller groups were perceived as membership roles. He must know his job, work harder then the rest, and have certain organising skills such as giving information to the members, allowing no exceptions to the rules, telling them what to do, etc. Thus members deal with their own inadequacy by welcoming a more directive type of leadership behaviour. A leader who 'gives the group a lead' allows members to sit back and make fewer contributions and still feel satisfied with the performance of the group. But this can only come about when the members feel that the leader has more to contribute than they have. Similarly, Hurwitz shows that at a social worker conference certain members were recognised by the groups as experts and the other members inhibited their own contributions to hear what the expert had to say.[1] It is worth while for our purpose to quote Carl Rogers (1951) at length at this point:

'Some counselors—usually those with little specific training—have supposed that the counsellor's role was merely to be passive and to adopt a *laissez-faire* policy. . . . He is more inclined to listen than to guide. He tries to avoid imposing his own evaluations upon the client. He finds that a number of his clients gain help for themselves. He feels that his faith in his client's capacity is best exhibited by a passivity which involves a minimum of activity and of emotional reaction on his part. He tries "to stay out of his client's way".

'This misconception of the approach has led to considerable failure in counseling—and for good reasons. In the first place, the passivity and seeming lack of interest or involvement is experienced by the client as a rejection, since indifference is in no real way the same as acceptance. In the second place a *laissez-faire* attitude does not in any way indicate to the client that he is regarded as a person of worth. . . . Many clients will leave both disappointed in their failure to receive help and disgusted with the counselor for having nothing to offer' (p. 27).

This is one of the many fields in which Kurt Lewin was a pioneer. Because of the nature of group influence, one man finds it difficult to stand out against the group. If it is possible to make a group understand the need for a change, then the group will discuss the situation and propose suitable changes, without resentment. To share in the adaptive phase brings about a unity of norms with the happy effect

[1] See page 31.

noted in the previous chapter.[1] Lewin (1952) provides many examples of this process. He has demonstrated how the discussion of food values, of work practices, and of group prejudice allows culturally approved decisions to be taken by the members and is a much more effective agent of change than are policies handed down from above. The members feel personally involved; the information they are given makes them desire a change. Often the *ad hoc* discussion groups turn into more permanent friendly groups. The increased interaction between the members brings about a closer unity of norms than would otherwise have been the case, and this makes possible the evolution of an informal system of control in which all members reinforce for one another the decision they took together.

There are special techniques to elicit from members the opinions and suggestions which they might otherwise withhold. The effect of Maier's technique, which we discussed at length in Chapter One is to ensure participation in adaptation and decision-making. It is not really important whether the leader is appointed or has emerged from the group, provided this function is fulfilled. He will be characterised by the great number of requests he makes for opinions or expressions of feeling (in particular Bales' three categories, 7, 8 and 9 may all be much used) and the amount of encouragement and agreement he shows (i.e. Bales' categories 1, 2 and 3).

It is interesting to note that Fromm (1942) differentiates between 'inhibiting authorities', leaders who, as interaction continues, sharpen the distinction between other members and themselves, and 'rational authorities', leaders who with continued interaction seek to minimise that distinction. The adaptive relationship should be of this latter kind. As Fromm characterises the former as authoritarian and the latter as democratic, we may note the correspondence of his terminology to that of Lippitt, Lewin and White.[2]

If a leader builds up a hierarchy culminating in himself, he will, with an increase in the size of the group, have to exercise more direct control. His other choice is to delegate some work and devise a division of labour, thereby encouraging communication between members. A picture will show that this inevitably makes the leader less central and therefore tends to obliterate the leader-follower distinction.

The issue here is really that of making the group perform at its

[1] See page 115.   [2] See page 101.

best level, encouraging the members to give out all the information they have at their disposal, pooling the resources of the group. The member who can produce this effect in the group has what Bales

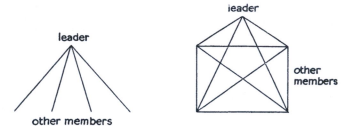

calls indirect access to resources—he has access to the resources of others. Once again Bales includes in his formula the giving of and asking for suggestions; we exclude it for the same reasons as before. The indirect access to resources of the ith member is indicated by the following formula:

$$\frac{(\bar{a} + {}_i)}{(\bar{a} + {}_i) + (a - {}_i)} \times \frac{(\bar{a} + {}_i)}{A+} \times 100$$

In words, the indirect access to resources of the ith member is indicated by the number of answers he receives in the categories of communication and evaluation plus the number of questions he asks in these categories, expressed as a fraction of the number of answers he receives (i.e. what proportion of his questions are answered), weighted by the total number of answers the group has given (i.e. how many answers were directed at others and not at i), the whole expressed as a percentage.[1]

---

[1] For this brief chapter no summary has been thought necessary.

CHAPTER TEN

Decision-making as Instrumental Behaviour: The Dimension of Control

WE have now discussed expressive behaviour and adaptive behaviour. In expressive behaviour the underlying values of the members are made manifest; during adaptive behaviour information is accumulated. Values and knowledge together form the frame of reference in terms of which an action or a person is preferred to another in a given set of circumstances. Often the values are thought of as goals; goals are values seen from the standpoint of what is to be achieved. But the decision to work for a goal is affected not only by its goodness in an absolute sense—by its value—but also by the knowledge of its feasibility; more simply, the decision to work for a goal is affected both by the system of knowledge and by the value system. The frame of reference may be regarded more concretely as a system of goals. These goals stand in a relationship to one another which enables one to see some goals as means, sub-goals or steps to other goals; goals determine what means shall be used. Thus an action is evaluated not only in terms of leading to 'the' goal, but also in terms of its effect, favourable or adverse, on other goals in the whole organised frame of reference.

The kind of behaviour now to be discussed has been variously called instrumental, conative, and goal-oriented. What are the common elements of these terms? According to the *Concise Oxford Dictionary*, *instrumental*—serving as an instrument or means, *conation*—the exertion of willing that desire or aversion may issue in action, (*goal*) *oriented*—*figuratively* bring into a clearly understood relation (with goal). From this semantic examination it is as clear as from the logical analysis in the previous paragraph that a means-end relationship is under consideration: that aspect of behaviour in which

K   129 knowledge (gained in the adaptive phase) is used to achieve a value (controlled by the expressive phase).[1]

The two relevant categories in Bales' observation schedule are 'control' (the making of and asking for suggestion) and 'decision' (agreeing or disagreeing with the suggestion). Here we differ very slightly from Bales. In the category of 'control' we put all suggestions and directions as to what shall be done and who shall do it. Unlike Bales we include the giving of definite orders. Whether such suggestions are followed up and whether the commands are obeyed is shown in the category of 'decision'. Thus the phase of 'control' involves only a *proposal* to act in a certain way. For this reason, and because we shall use the word control for a different kind of behaviour, we shall call Bales' category of 'control' that of 'proposal'. A proposal to act will only be acted upon if it is followed by positive reactions in the category of 'decision', which we shall call the category of 'agreement', for it shows that the group has agreed to a proposal. Control is exercised to bring such agreement about.

It is clear that we are not concerned with knowing whether a goal has been achieved and indeed Bales' observation scheme is not designed to describe whether an action has been carried out or not, nor whether the goals are good or bad, nor whether the means are efficient or inefficient. It can only show how often proposals have been made and how much agreement they could secure. What we are measuring is measurable only up to the point where the group acts, it cannot tell us about the action itself. Clearly then, the important aspects of this kind of behaviour lie in the making of proposals and the securing of agreement, with steps toward goals, with plans of action. For that reason we propose to describe it by the term 'decision-making' rather than by the terms previously suggested.

In analysing the decision-making process the structural characteristics of the group come out very clearly, especially as they relate to a shared frame of reference and to the distribution of power. Since action is taken with reference to goals, the important question to ask is, are the goals of all members taken into account or only the goals

---

[1] We may say at this point that expressive behaviour is goal-related and only remotely task-related, that adaptive behaviour is task-related and only remotely goal-related, and that the two categories of 'control' (making and asking for suggestions) and 'decision' (agreeing or disagreeing) which form the subject of the present chapter are equally goal-related and task-related. The further away the observation categories from the category of adaptation the more goal-related and the less task-related they become; see also page 146.

of some, or more simply, who controls? The decision-making process comes to an end, not when the best means to the best goals have been chosen, but when the group agrees on a course of action. This will depend on two sets of variables which we shall combine and recombine: whether all members share in decision-making or not (i.e. who controls) and whether they share a frame of reference or not. Between them, these define progress towards goals.[1]

ASSUMPTION ONE

Let all members participate in decision-making and let them share a frame of reference.

Let us recall a distinction between two types of tasks that we made in the first chapter of this book. The task may be such that when a course of action is proposed it is so obviously the correct procedure that members cannot but agree. The problem is solved as soon as communication and evaluation have led to a full understanding.[2] The major phase has been that of adaptation. The first proposal of action is at once followed by agreement. Decision-making is not difficult in those circumstances. This may happen in such tasks as mechanical puzzles—how can we make the bell ring, in crossword puzzles, and in other problems with demonstrably correct solutions. Where there is no demonstrable solution, it will take longer to come to a conclusion unless members share a frame of reference to such an extent that certain things seem more or less self-evident to them. Although there is no demonstrable proof of the existence of God, a group of Christians would at once agree that He does exist. The more similar the members' frames of reference are, the less time it will take for a group to come to a decision, even when problems with no demonstrable solution are in question. Thus the length of time devoted to decision-making is a fair indication of the degree to which a group shares a frame of reference, provided that all members share in the decision-making process. In a group that has existed for some time

[1] It may be noted that the group may face two different kinds of task. It may be a task which is ended when all members are agreed. Such a task would be the appointment of a leader or the equitable distribution of reward. In this case the problem is to get agreement—agreement *is* the solution of the problem—it *is* the goal. The other kind of task involves the actual handling of materials, the modification of the environment. In that case the group's problem is twofold. (1) To get agreement on a plan of action which will *bring about* a solution of the problem; and (2) to carry out the plan.

[2] Note that this is not a 'fully-fledged' problem in Bales' sense of the word; see page 17.

and in which interaction has been general, this condition is likely to come about.

Let all members participate in decision-making and let the group not share a frame of reference.

In many circumstances, groups are faced with the problem of making a decision—committing themselves to a course of action—when norms in the group are less uniformly shared than we supposed under the previous assumption.

When different members have different norms, they will not be able to agree on what is the best way to cope with a problem because each sees the problem in a different context according to his individual frame of reference. It is at the point of decision that differences show up and prolong the period of decision-making. A proposal will be rejected because it does not fit into what a man believes to be the correct perspective. At this point control comes into play. Somehow the members must induce one another to co-operate in the execution of a task. The process of control aims at getting the members to co-operate even when they are not very anxious to do so. In a group which operates under functional authority, the discussion will at this point revert to the adaptive phase. This reversion has the function of making explicit the frames of reference of members, showing up the sources of disagreement and enabling matters of context to be thrashed out. This may suffice.

It may suffice, but adaptive behaviour presupposes a degree of rationality in the group members which is often little short of the Utopian. Fortunately, the group in which there is much interaction and in which all members participate in making the decision—a group in which there is functional authority, in short—has a second means of control. Members who might not be amenable to influence on the adaptive level may change their norms, consciously or not, for friendship's sake. If neither reversion to the adaptive phase nor the friendly influence of other members brings a deviant into agreement with a proposed course of action, withdrawal of friendship and of interaction may have the desired effect.

In Chapter Six we showed that the group does influence the individual; we will now show how it does so. We need not spend much time on this because Homans (1950) has a chapter on social control to which we can add nothing further. According to him: 'The members of a group are obedient to its norms not only because they have actually disobeyed and been punished in the past, but also because they see what would happen if they did disobey. They may not think of the relationships of the social system in the same way as we do, but they are nevertheless effectively aware of the relationships and are therefore able to anticipate the consequences of breaking a rule' (pp. 292–3). Thus either the first signs of a withdrawal of friendship or of interaction (we may call them, with Homans, *virtual changes*), or the anticipation of such a withdrawal, controls the behaviour of members. Of course, one cannot demonstrate this; one can only see the evidence of successful control in such behaviour as was described in Chapter Six. If control is unsuccessful, one can see the withdrawal of friendship and interaction. This aspect is very beautifully demonstrated in an experiment by Schachter (1950), in which three people were instructed to behave to a fourth, naïve, subject in the following ways. One, the *deviate*, was instructed to take a position in the discussion that was markedly different from that of the naïve subject, and to maintain this position throughout the discussion. A second, the *slider*, was instructed to start in the same way as the deviate, but to allow himself to be persuaded to change his position and to come to agree with the naïve subject. The third, the *mode*, was instructed to agree with the naïve subject from the beginning. After a period of intense interaction with the *deviate*, to be interpreted as an attempt to change the other's mind, the naïve subject ceased to talk with him; to all intents and purposes the *deviate* ceased to be a member of the group. A sociometric questionnaire at the end of the discussion showed that the *deviate* was least liked by the naïve subject. (N.B. In spite of the period of intense interaction.) As interaction with the *deviate* decreased interaction between the naïve subject, the *slider* and the *mode* became more general. Still, the *mode* was preferred to the *slider* in the sociometric test.[1]

[1] We have discussed the case where norms are similar and interaction general, and the case where norms are different and the group splits. Let us now consider an intermediate case. Members A, B and C are related in the following way. A has a set of norms some of which he shares with B. Communication between them, though difficult at times, is possible. B and C also share certain norms and can communicate. But A and C share no norms. They are incomprehensible to one another. In this case B serves a very useful function. He can transmit between A and C, 'translating' as he goes along. In this way he makes it possible for A and C to co-operate in the performance of a task. Without him the group would split. A situation of this kind was experimentally produced by Festinger, Gerard, *et al.* (1952). It is therefore possible

If deviance is displayed not by one member, but a set of members sharing a set of norms, control by group pressure is less possible. Conversely, persons who are unwilling to be controlled by one another, because they cannot agree that the others' proposals are the best ones, will try to form schismatic sub-groups. We showed in Chapters Seven and Eight how conformity to a particular norm brings popularity from others who also subscribe to this norm. Where there is more than one set of norms in the group there will be more than one popularity cluster. And since these members will tend to interact more among themselves than with members of other sub-groups, even interaction in the adaptive dimension is likely to prove ineffective.

Whether we discuss deviant individuals or deviant sub-groups, the result is inevitably a reduction in interaction with those members of the group who hold other norms. In the case of the deviant individual this reduction in interaction may be painful to him and he may correct his norms in order to regain the group's good graces. In the case of a deviant sub-group this is less likely to happen because the deviant members will support one another; the fear of isolation does not operate so strongly here. Thus norms define cliques and separate one group from another.

Since deviance from the norms of others may cause these others to withdraw their friendship and/or to interact with them less frequently, the more cohesive the group is, the greater the control that can be exercised this way. The less friendly groups, in which interaction is in any case less frequent, cannot exert the same pressure on its members because they communicate less often. This will lead to individualistic actions by the members which would in turn cut them off still further from group influence. In the course of this process the individual will be less susceptible to informal influence and control, and if other members do seek to influence him he will feel this as an external constraint and resent it. He is also more likely to have to be told what to do if his co-operation is needed for group purposes as he is not sufficiently well well-informed to see for himself

for members with very different points of view to communicate with one another provided that they are in a group with members whose norms range between the two extremes. Possibly this situation is a very unstable one, with both extremes recruiting adherents from the middle pool, or with the extremes gradually conforming more to the group norms. In the former case groups would evolve who were unwilling to communicate with one another.

what needs doing. Formal control is therefore likely to be applied to him more frequently than to those 'more in the know'. The less attached a member is, the sooner control is likely to be exerted on him and the sooner he will leave if he comes under such a pressure. At the very extreme, communication between him and other members may be so inadequate that he is even unaware of the pressure to change.

When the whole group shares in decision-making and there is an adequate period of discussion, control tends to work through making the norms of members more similar rather than through the manipulation of definite rewards. Since a learning process is involved, however, we may say that there is a kind of reward, namely, acceptance by the group.

ASSUMPTION THREE

Let members share a frame of reference in a group in which not all members participate in making the decision.

The fact that the group shares a frame of reference should tell us who will be the leader, the man who makes the decisions. Whenever members share a common frame of reference they will be friendly. We have noted that tightly-knit groups of friends can make demands upon one another that would be resented in other kinds of small groups.[1] This is because the control exercised in such groups is not experienced as an external constraint. It is an imperceptible control, operating through *internalised* standards, and it brings high status for that member who best exemplifies those standards. He is able to elicit the response he desires from others because they respect him for what he is. In groups of this kind, no hostility will be generated by the control that keeps the group in being.

At this point we may continue a discussion which we left off at the end of Chapter Three. If members share a frame of reference, there may be differences in status, but these will be willingly acknowledged and maintained by the members themselves. Because they admire their leader they will be gladly under his authority. Status differences and all that they imply are therefore not always resented.

---

[1] For one thing, as Bovard has shown, they know which are the norms which are so valuable to other members that they must not deviate from them, and in which areas of behaviour greater divergences are permitted. In this sense the members of a very close group feel more free from group pressures than members of less intensely interacting groups.

Members are content with their low status and consequent lack of control if their position is congruent with their own evaluation of relative worth. Hurwitz and his fellow workers, for instance, in the study mentioned on page 31, report no expression of resentment from low-status members at the social worker conference. Mary Parker Follett made it clear that the division of labour and consequent restriction on freedom of action need not create resentment *although* it involves the process of control.[1] This will be so when there is a general agreement about the status of every member and a belief in the right of other members to set about the task in their own way.

Where the values of the group are subscribed to by all the members, those members will have high status—i.e. the ability to elicit the response they desire—who best exemplify those values. There is therefore a kind of leadership in which the leader, by representing most fully the values of the members, is able to control them because they recognise the justice of his demands. Such a man will be identifiable by the large number of acceptable suggestions he makes. The formula for a member x would be:

$$\frac{\text{proposals made by } x}{\substack{\text{total proposals made and} \\ \text{asked for in the group}}} \times \frac{\text{agreement received by } x}{\substack{\text{total agreement and dis-} \\ \text{agreement in the group}}}$$

It may be noted as a matter of interest that what we are saying here is not so far removed from Freud's analysis of the leader as the super-ego of the group.[2]

[1] See page 19.

[2] Control cannot be exercised if those who wish to control are too different from those who are to be controlled. Early studies on leadership qualities have accordingly and quite rightly stressed that whereas the leader would be superior in some ways to his followers, a man who was too greatly superior to his fellow-members would not be a leader. He has no way of making himself easily understood by them. In this way, we may say, the leader is himself controlled by the group. He cannot afford to be too different and to depart too radically from the norms of the group.

Once again we repeat it. People are willing to be controlled without question only by those to whom they attribute their personality-ideal. Such men must be better than they are, but still within the same range. They must be better, but not too different, because then they will not correspond to what the members have hopes of becoming. Thus Festinger (1954):

'Given a range of possible persons for comparison, some one close to one's own ability or opinion will be chosen for comparison.' 'If the only comparison available is a very divergent one, the person will not be able to make a subjectively precise evaluation of his opinion or ability,' and 'When a discrepancy exists with respect to opinions or abilities there will be tendencies to cease comparing oneself with those in the group who are very different from oneself.'

Clearly, therefore, when norms are shared and the leaders are known to exemplify those norms better than others do, the leaders will be seen as 'knowing best' in a very real sense. They will be trusted whether or not the others understood the reason for which the decision from which they were excluded was made. This trust may also be created from past interaction in the adaptive dimension. It will be remembered that some tasks bring about a distinction between central and peripheral positions. The peripheral members communicate with one another through the central members. Even when initially all members are assumed to have equivalent bits of information, the central members possess more information than the others in the middle stages of the problem-solving process, since what they are transmitting has not yet reached its final destination. If the central members are also in the position of important open cells, information about the environment will reach them before it reaches the others and the decision they take on the strength of their information may be puzzling to other members until the relevant information has been relayed to them.

When decisions have to be made in a hurry, the decisions of the central members are more likely to be right than those of other members, since they possessed more information at the time when the decision had to be taken. They thus create a trust in themselves on the strength of previous successes. They are privileged by what Barnard (1938) calls a 'zone of indifference', which enables them to make decisions which will be accepted even though other members do not understand the reason for the decision.

Moreover, members in central positions gain experience in their function as co-ordinators, which is not open to other members.[1] Where a group is relatively short-lived such structural consequences are not likely to be very important, but in a group that has existed for some time the recurrence of these middle phases is likely to endow the central members with influence at other times than when the peculiarities of the network justify it, or on occasions when the possession of information would not *eo ipse* be a determinant of influence. Group members get into the habit of obedience.[2]

[1] See page 48.
[2] Disagreement as to what shall be done may be the result of ignorance rather than a lack of desire to please. A member may transmit information at his disposal and make a suggestion on the basis of what he knows, only to find that it is not acceptable to the group. The reason for this may be in the fact that other members do not suffi-

Let the decision-making function be restricted to certain members of the group in a group where there is no shared frame of reference. In many circumstances the leader or the ruling élite may have norms different from those of other members of the group. In such circumstances differences in status will obviously lead to misunderstanding because the leaders' perspective is not understood by the members. Whether a giver of information is understood by his recipient depends therefore on the frames of reference of both parties. It is not purely a matter of good patterns of communication. Moreover, if there is disagreement about norms, there will be disagreement about the proper course of action. Control will be resented because the restriction on one's freedom of action is felt to have been imposed from the outside. In such situations, communication is likely to be inefficient; and at the same time commands and proposals will be felt to spring from the arbitrary authority of the leader and not from the logic of the situation—although in the leader's eye of course they may do so. Control is often distributed in such a way that not all members are satisfied. Then we get hostile reactions from low-status members. In this way, Thibaut accounts for the hostility that his low-status groups manifest toward those who perform the more attractive tasks.[1]

Let us now consider Homans' generalisation that 'when two persons interact with one another, the more frequently one originates interaction for the other, the stronger the latter's attitude of respect or hostility towards him.'[2] Can we know in what circumstances the origination of interaction is accompanied by respect and when by hostility? It should be clear now that it will evoke hostility when members are not agreed about the status of him who originates the action or when the tasks they are given are felt to be both disagreeable and arbitrary. When the members lack information, or

ciently understand the frame of reference by which the proposal was regulated. Highly active members tend in any case to support one another and they may be genuinely unaware that the more remote or more silent members do not understand or approve. It is therefore important for the expert to carry other members with him through the process of adaptation and to allow them to make their own proposals and secure their own agreement, if a decision acceptable to all is to be reached. But with this subject we have already dealt fairly fully; see pages 125–128.

[1] See page 101, and also Sherif (1951).
[2] Homans would now prefer to use the phrase 'originating *action*'. (private communication.)

when they do not share the norms of the originator of action to a sufficient extent to feel that the proposed course of action is a necessary one, they will feel that the control over their actions has been arbitrarily imposed.[1] When, on the other hand, the members do share a set of norms to which the originator of the action corresponds most closely and when the members have sufficient information to understand at least to some extent why the action is necessary, he will naturally be respected.

If the leader is the chief agent of decision he may find himself in a difficult position. We have shown in a previous chapter how a popular man may find himself in a position of leadership. But once he starts making decisions for other members he grows apart from them; they may no longer see eye to eye with him and they will resent his control accordingly. In this way we may account for the fact, previously noted in Chapter Seven, that it is not the man who makes the most suggestions and is recognised as having good ideas who is the most popular.

The leader's position may be made easier in a number of ways.

1. Heinecke and Bales have shown that once the struggle for status is won, the leader may exercise control through his lieutenants. By this means he is able to preserve both his power and his popularity.[2]

2. Where there is no shared frame of reference, decisions are most quickly reached in a highly centralised group, where central members have sufficient knowledge, influence or trust to carry out their decisions regardless of the state of opinion in the group. Restricted interaction patterns may be deliberately created or they may come about by accident. Bad communication often goes together with the exclusion of some members from the decision-making process and with differences in the norms of members. Whether such restriction will be resented depends on whether the norms are generally shared although the members do not realise it, or whether the leading subgroup has norms of its own. Even where it is resented, the interaction pattern will tend to inhibit the expression of resentment. Where there are great differences in centrality, the peripheral members cannot communicate, or can only communicate with great difficulty. They cannot therefore find out the strength of their numbers, and

---

[1] One may suspect that a number of joint-consultation ventures fail for precisely this reason.

[2] See pages 105-106.

they cannot conspire to overthrow or disobey the edicts from on high, because they can only communicate through the central members.

3. Members of groups are all too prone to turn apathetic and they may not sufficiently resist the attempts of others to gain control of the group. The leader will serve as a scapegoat. He can be blamed if things go wrong. Their own attitude to responsibility is therefore likely to be apathetic. They may resent it in others but they fear to take it up for themselves. This tendency is likely to be accelerated in times of crisis. 'As crisis continues, dominant power increases both in scope and in weight' (Lasswell and Kaplan, 1951, p. 224). The demand for urgent action tends to put the weight of decision-making on the shoulders of those highly thought of in the group. Lasswell and Kaplan go on to say:

'The demand for resolution of the crisis acts on the predispositions set up by these identifications (with the leader) to strengthen, initially at least, faith in the leadership. An element of charisma may come into play to offset insecurity: there is no limit to what the leader can accomplish with the weight of power in his hands. This pressure is reinforced by the demands made by the self on the self: to relinquish the share of power is to acquit the self of responsibility. There are involved also expectations of expediency. Crisis is taken to impose restrictions on the process of decision-making which necessitate more and more participation in the process by fewer and fewer power-holders.'

Thus restriction of the decision-making function is accentuated by environmental pressure. At the same time the more urgent the problem the less likely it is that the whole elaborate process of information-seeking, evaluation and decision by all members of the group will be gone through. The division of labour will become rather rigid. Control will become more important, and therefore status differentiation also. The structure will become more centralised so that high-status members can take upon themselves the task of evaluation and decision. In this way the number of members that have to be persuaded of the correctness of a value-judgement will be reduced and this aspect of the task will take less time. The more urgent the problem the more likely it is that the group will restrict its communication pattern.

4. The effects of an urgent survival problem are also induced by an increase in the size of the group. We have seen that when the group is large there are members who are diffident in expressing themselves. The influence of the leader is much more marked in these circumstances. The larger group carries within it the seeds of organisation. Members themselves seem to sense that leadership is different in the larger group—they expect the leader to be more autocratic and, even, more arbitrary.[1] Thus the fact that agreement is more difficult in the larger group is offset by the fact that an oligarchy tends to develop in any case and this reduces the number of members who have to be consulted when proposals for action are being considered.

SUMMARY

(1) 'Instrumental', 'conative', 'goal-oriented' behaviour is concerned with decision-making.

(2) Decision-making involves making proposals and securing agreement.

(3) In some cases agreement is the goal of the group; in other cases agreement leads to action which is designed to secure the goal.

(4) Decision-making involves a power-dimension because it may have to be secured by means of controlling other members.

(5) If all members share a set of norms, decisions are held up only by lack of information.

(6) If all members share in decision-making but differ in norms, decision making is prolonged and group pressure is exerted to secure uniformity of norms.

(7) If sub-groups differ in norms, group pressure on the deviant sub-groups is less likely to be successful and a struggle for supremacy may take place.

(8) If decision-making is restricted to some members of the group:

    (a) other members will respond with respect if the group shares norms; differences in status and control will not be resented because the values are internalised;

    (b) other members will respond with hostility when norms are

[1] See page 127.

not shared or, in groups with restricted communication, not known to be shared.

(9) Marked differences in centrality and peripherality are likely to occur when the pressure of the environment produces a rigid organisation.

(10) In a group with marked differences between central and peripheral members, the peripheral members are likely to have little power and little information. A relationship of trust from them to the central members may develop when norms are shared or the central members' proposals have been successful in the past.

CHAPTER ELEVEN

The Self-defeating Process:
Latent Pattern Maintenance

IN this book many relationships have been stated between the factors which affect the behaviour of members of small groups. Whenever attempts at such statements are made, two methodological problems have ultimately to be faced, and these two problems in a well-organised science, should come to the same thing. The first question is: 'What relationships exist between those elements used for analysis whose relationship has not been explicitly stated?' The second question is: 'Why don't two directly varying factors, such as, for instance, increasing friendship and increasing interaction, go on for ever?' The answer to both questions is the same. Variables A and B do not mutually encourage one another to infinity, because a relationship exists between A and X, and B and X, which inhibits the mutual influence of A and B beyond a particular point. Any ambitious sociologist would wish to put forward a system in which relationships can be as clearly stated as this, and the time may be very near when it can be done in the limited field of small group studies. In this chapter we attempt to carry this ambition a little further.

The question we ask ourselves in this chapter is: how does the group survive? Before we can answer this question we must ask ourselves another. What does it mean to say: 'a group survives'?

Survival means at least the following two things: the group remains distinct from its environment—it can be recognised by others as a separate unit—and the group maintains some kind of continuity in the qualities by virtue of which it is recognised as separate. More concretely this means, first, that members interact with one another more than any outsider does, and second, that the norms of the group change relatively slowly—it is by virtue of its particular norms that the group is recognisable as being the same at two points of time.

A group has to make efforts in order to survive: it has to change the environment when necessary, to adapt itself to the environment when it cannot change it, to distribute rewards so that members will remain in the group and so on. Such efforts at survival can be described in more general terms than we have so far employed; they can be described in terms of the survival of a system. A set of units is a system when each unit affects every other unit in the set to an extent greater than some arbitrarily established lower limit.[1]

We have been careful throughout this book to define a group in such a way that it is a system. A man is a member of a group if he interacts more within the group in question than with the other groups which form the environment, and he must interact with all members so that his behaviour affects theirs and theirs affects his. We shall now go further and assume that the group is a system in some kind of equilibrium, that is to say, we assume that the group is a system of such a kind that it is able to minimise the effect of disruptive forces which might change the group. The assumption of general equilibrium is no more than an assumption, there is not sufficient evidence in the literature to take it as established. There is, however, no doubt that there are what we may call equilibrating mechanisms, processes which operate in such a way as to limit other processes which might, if unchecked, radically change the nature of the group, or even destroy the group altogether.

There are many group processes whose function, either main or incidental, is to keep the group as far as possible in its present state. In order to describe such equilibrating mechanisms we shall often assume that, of the large number of factors which between them determine the nature of group processes, only two are changing, while all the others remain constant and unaffected by the temporary state of the two on which we fix our attention. This is perhaps a rather unrealistic assumption to make, but it is as much as we are entitled to do. We shall also find that it is not always useful to think in terms of an equilibrium point. We shall very often find that, instead, control operates in such a way that when the dangerous trend is checked, the group process is deflected into the 'opposite

[1] See also the discussion in Chapter Four, page 49 and page 51.

144

direction' until it in turn becomes dangerous and is once more reversed.[1]

We are supposing that there are a number of trends in the group which, if they were allowed to continue unchecked, would eventually disrupt the group, and that there are other group processes which operate in such a way that they limit the dangerous operation of such trends and bring the group back to a safer state.

The general principle on which this oscillation operates—it is a kind of feedback—we will call the self-defeating process. An analogy will make our meaning clear. Yeast grows when put into a sugar-solution. Whilst it grows, it produces alcohol as a by-product. Eventually it produces so much alcohol that it cannot survive. The alcohol kills the yeast. Our argument is that a group, in performing a certain activity, inevitably produces side-effects which hinder the performance of that activity to such an extent that, if the group is to survive, it must switch its attention and its activity to deal with the side-effects. In doing so, further effects are produced which in turn will ultimately present problems so pressing that the group's attention must now switch to activity that will deal with them.

We have already become familiar with such sequences in earlier chapters without using our new concept of the self-defeating process specifically. It will be remembered, for instance, that a popular man will find that he is able to control the group. If he exercises that control for some time, he will tend to lose his popularity. Or again, a group of friends works hard to survive in an environment that has become uncongenial. By concentrating on the task, the friendship level of the group will tend to drop.

We must now determine which types of behaviour in the group are related in such a way that within a limit they support one another, and that when they transgress that limit they hinder one another and disrupt the group. These must be many, but we shall confine ourselves to three. These three in turn derive from Bales' categories which we have already used.

We have now completed our modification of Bales' scheme. The new scheme is reproduced below.

[1] A very interesting and valuable contribution along these lines was made by Simon in 1952. He uses what is for our science a highly sophisticated mathematical technique in order to work out how a slight change along one dimension will affect behaviour in others, on Homans' basis of the relationships between interaction, friendship and norms.

	Expressive behaviour:	irrelevant friendly, rewarding, cohesive behaviour.
positive	Decision-making:	(a) making proposals for action.
		(b) agreeing to proposals.
	Adaptive behaviour:	communication and evaluation.

	Adaptive behaviour:	requests for information (communication and evaluation).
negative	Decision-making:	(a) asking for proposals for action.
		(b) disagreeing with proposals made.
	Expressive behaviour:	irrelevant, hostile, unrewarding, disruptive behaviour.

adaptive behaviour		*task related.*
decision-making	*(a) proposals*	*task related.*
	(b) agreement	*goal related.*
expressive behaviour		*goal related.*

This chapter derives several of its ideas from the *Working Papers in the Theory of Action*, in which Bales combines with Parsons and Shils in an attempt to enlarge the scope of his theory. Here again we select only those aspects which are of interest to our argument and once again we modify and amplify unscrupulously when it suits us. The reader must not expect to find this chapter a substitute for reading the *Working Papers*.[1]

One of the contributions that that book makes is to define the three categories of adaptation, goal achievement and expressive behaviour as *dimensions* along which the group process may be evaluated. Any activity in which the group engages may be seen as progress (or regress) along one or more of the dimensions, which are therefore measuring-rods indicating changes in the group. Although the measuring-rods are assumed to be independent, this does not exclude the possibility that progress along one dimension necessitates changes along other dimensions. In the physical world, inches measure one thing and pounds another, but after a certain point

[1] It will be noticed that in this chapter we rely very much on the work of Parsons, Bales and Shils; if we presume to criticise some of their views we do so with diffidence. Even if our criticism is ill-conceived, we need not worry too much. 'If his status is highest in the group, and he is the source of authority, it is as if he "can do no wrong", and disagreements from other members are taken simply as signals that they are confused, in error, or deviant. It is then the leader's job to "remain steadfast", and to correct the deviance by his own consistent attitude and administration of rewards and punishments. So long as his status is the highest in the group, his positive and negative responses function as rewards and punishments to the other members, but not vice versa' (Parsons, Bales and Shils (1953), p. 139).

taller people will tend to be heavier than short ones. Parsons, Bales and Shils seem to suggest in several places that the group-processes themselves are also independent of one another. Not only would it be very uninteresting if this were true, but their assumption is based on a confusion. Thus, e.g. on page 166 in the *Working Papers*:

'We have noted that a given amount of motivational energy cannot, at the same time, be both expended on an instrumental process (i.e. on decision-making) and "stored up" for later use: these are independent directions of its flow.'

But on page 167 they say: 'Every change of state of one unit . . . will affect all the other units in the system and in turn the effect of these effects on the other units will "feed back" to the original unit.' And again, page 190:

'Goal gratification and latency (a state in which the tensions which produce group processes are absent) then designate anti-thetical, i.e. *independent directions* of the disposal of the inflow of motivational energy into the system.'[1]

Plainly, however, a very firm although negatively related dependency is established between two variables which can on no account be found together. Such dependencies have very great value for prediction and deduction.

We shall assume that activity along one dimension may affect activity along other dimensions. We shall hope to find that progress along one dimension may create a situation in which that progress becomes self-defeating and comes to a standstill. It will be interesting and legitimate, therefore, to see exactly what happens to group processes when one of them is maximised at the expense of others.

ASSUMPTION ONE

Let progress in the adaptive dimension be maximised.

In the adaptive phase, the store of information at the disposal of the group is increased and improved. A group is in process of adaptation when information is being communicated and evaluated. Clearly, the process we are describing would in the individual be

---

[1] The brackets are inserted for explanatory purposes, since Parsons, Bales and Shils use a rather more detailed but for our purposes irrelevant classification. The italics, however, are by Parsons, Bales and Shils.

called 'learning'. To measure progress along this dimension would involve counting the amount of information possessed by the group (often only in so far as it relates to the immediate chances of survival, which is easy enough in experimental conditions at least) before and after any group act.

Adaptation is essentially a passive process. It does not change the environment and it changes the group only in so far as the acquisition of information may be called a change of state. But decisions depend on the available information and therefore adaptation affects decision-making. In a different way, decision-making affects adaptation. When a plan is being carried out, further information is fed back to the group about the results that are being achieved.

In the normal course of events the maximisation of adaptation comes to an end when someone, feeling that all relevant information is now in hand, makes a proposal for action and the group moves into the decision-making phase. If for one reason or another this does not occur, the maximisation in this phase still comes to an end. The dissatisfaction of the group with the present situation will manifest itself in expressive behaviour. When other activities have been neglected in the pursuit of learning, the tension rises to such an extent that the group must move to another phase of the sequence in order to reduce it.

ASSUMPTION TWO

Let decision-making be maximised.
The group is faced with successive problems which have to be solved if it is to survive. Decisions have to be taken as to how to deal with dangers. If we were to measure progress in this dimension we should analyse such a problem in terms of the succession of steps needed to reach a solution. The number of steps needed to reach the goal, before and after any group act, would indicate progress along this dimension.

Progress in decision-making is very simply and directly related to progress along the adaptive dimension. As each further step toward the goal is taken, more information about the effect of acting in this particular way is gained. That is to say, progress in the decision-making area brings progress in the adaptive dimension also. (Though not necessarily all that would have been learned, if learning had been the maximised activity.)

148

Success in decision-making is followed by positive reactions in the expressive category. The task would not have been selected by the group if the present situation had not been creating dissatisfaction. The fact that something is being done will in itself be satisfying to the members, and if the group achieves its goal, that will certainly be rewarding. In this way the cohesiveness of the group is strengthened. Failure in decision-making will either lead back to a search for further information, i.e. to the adaptive dimension, or to negative expressive behaviour, since decision-making may involve the members in more control than they like, and failure itself is often disruptive.

Behaviour in this dimension comes to an end, then, when success or failure leads naturally to one of the other two dimensions.

Let expressive behaviour be maximised.

The expressive dimension throws light on the cohesion of the group. When the emotion expressed is friendly, it provides satisfaction for the members; when it is hostile, it shows the dissatisfaction of members with the present activity of the group and tends to disrupt it. If the group satisfies the members, they will be less anxious to seek satisfactions (and to offer their services) elsewhere. Expressive behaviour manifests the extent to which the group is thought to hold out inducements for the individual. Two aspects have to be considered: intensity of interrelations inside the group, and the proportion of links within the group to those between the group and its environment. For this reason the traditional measure of cohesiveness—the ratio of ingroup to outgroup choices—may be used.

Expressive behaviour, though irrelevant to the task on the manifest level, shows the extent to which the group in its present activity is satisfying the members. All this was discussed in detail in Chapter Eight. Only one additional remark need be made. A goal may be far ahead, and when the energies of members flag and they become discouraged, friendly behaviour, reassurance, praise, jokes, will have an integrative function. It is mildly, though not permanently, tension-reductive.

We have shown how progress both in the adaptive and the decision-making directions may come to an end with expressive

149

behaviour. Tension expression is therefore a limiting condition for these two other activities. There are levels below which activity in other areas may not fall even when activity in one area is maximised, lest that activity defeat its own object. If it does fall below this level, the expression of dissatisfaction abruptly brings the maximisation of the current activity to a stop.

Expressive behaviour itself is limited in the same way. In the course of such behaviour, whether friendly or hostile, no progress is made in the task, nor is anything learned. It is therefore again a self-defeating process. It comes to a stop when the environment becomes so disagreeable that the group must either break up or switch its activity into more profitable channels. If too much time is spent on group morale the task won't get done or the group will become isolated from its surroundings and have no interaction in any but the expressive areas.

LATENT PATTERN MAINTENANCE

We may now draw some conclusions about the way in which interaction operates in the group.

'As we shall think of the matter, when the articulation of any of these aspects fails for any reason to be adequate to maintain or support the ongoing process as a total stream or where affect is sufficiently strong, there is a sudden modification of the cognitive-affective-conative stream or process directed toward a mending or further development of the deficient aspects or an expression of the surplus affect. The deficiency or surplus removed, the stream modifies to mend another deficiency or to overcome another barrier to its free flow. The acts which we conceptually isolate and observe are these sudden modifications of the total stream, and our classification of them is in terms of the deficiency or surplus we judge to be present, or the kind of support to the ongoing process which they offer, or the kind of barrier they remove (not in terms of what they 'are') (Bales, 1951, pp. 52, 53).

In our terminology we would say that the period in which any one of the categories of adaptations, or decision-making, or expressive behaviour is maximised, comes to an end when the group perceives the need to switch over to interaction of a different category. If the group fails to perceive the need to change the kind of interaction in which it engages, it meets the problem of survival—either of the survival of the group or of the survival of the kind of group which it has hitherto been. The kind of group which it has hitherto been we shall call the latent pattern of the group. The latent pattern—that which distinguishes it from its environment and makes it a unique phenomenon, one might say gives it its integrity—is therefore a system in equilibrium.

Often the expression of tension is the equilibrating mechanism. Tension-expression operates in the same way as pain does in the human body: it gives a warning so that the disease may be corrected before it has gone too far. When, in the adaptive phase, members show that they are getting tired of just talking round the problem; or when, in the period of decision-making, they show their impatience of those who will not agree or with the fact that they are basing decisions on guesswork, the expression of tension ushers in a change in the type of interaction engaged in by the group. In a group with more sophisticated or experienced members, the advent of tension may be foreseen, of course, and then the interaction changes before tension rises high. This foresight may limit the expression of tension itself. When, in the expressive phase, members get frightened of their own aggression or begin to feel dissatisfied with doing nothing except being together, they will seek a task to do.

Thus, although an impairment is often first signalled by expressive behaviour, any kind of interaction may at times reduce tension. The maintenance of the latent pattern involves a particular relationship between adaptation, decision-making, and expressive behaviour. The proper balance between them reduces tension and maintains the latent pattern of the group. (Latent pattern maintenance is therefore not on the same level of abstraction as the other categories, as is implied in the *Working Papers*.)

Thus either the ongoing process flows sweetly from knowledge to action and satisfaction, in which case no tension need be expressed, or dissatisfaction with any particular phase compels the group to alter the direction of its activity. It should also be clear now that tension, or perhaps one would prefer to call it the expression of dis- satisfaction, is not the undesirable phenomenon it is so often thought to be. It, or the threat of it, is a precondition for all activity. The dis- crepancy between the state of the group and the state of the environ- ment leads to tension. If this tension did not exist, there would be no

151

group goal, no learning, and in fact no group, for the group would be indistinguishable from its environment.[1]

[1] An improper balance between the dimensions in which the group operates is not the only threat to equilibrium. A new recruit is likely to precipitate difficulties in the group. If a man joins a group because he likes certain of its norms, he will prefer good conformers to others. He is also more susceptible to their influence: he is more likely to do what they ask him, than what other members whom he does not respect so much, ask him to do. In order to retain their friendship and not to be cut off from them, he will accede to their requests. He will value their friendship more highly than that of members who are less strong in their conformity to his values. By this means he has changed the balance of power in the group and his faction will be able to exert more power on the relatively deviant groups. We showed in Chapter Ten that this pressure may defeat its own object.

There is another way in which a new recruit may change the balance of power in the group. He may have joined the group because he likes some of the members he knows. But the norms of the members he knows may be slightly different from those of others in the group. He is more susceptible to their influence than to the influence of other members, and he has increased the weight of a 'deviant' sub-group. As a result a struggle for supremacy of control, or rather for a supremacy of values, may take place, and the group may split into sub-groups. If unity is itself one of the norms shared by both sub-groups great efforts will be made to come to an agreement (and during this time much interaction may take place between the sub-groups, which may itself be a means of patching up the split). If the attempts are unsuccessful the group will split. There is, of course, a third possibility. The task may be so important that the group cannot afford to split. That is to say, the rewards of achievement may be sufficient to keep the members within the group.

When the balance of power shifts with the advent of a new recruit, other members may find themselves in a worse position than before. The balance of rewards and disadvantages may shift so that there is no longer a sufficient inducement for some members to stay in the group unless they are given further rewards. But one of the weightiest rewards which the group creates for its members is the use of the group for ends important to the self. Group life involves not only the manipulation of the environment but also the manipulation of other members of the group. A man may decide that he has the solution to the problems which face the group, but finds himself unable to persuade the group of the rightness of his views. Since he needs the group in order to carry out his plans he cannot leave but must instead endeavour to gain control over at least some of the members. Then he will find himself involved in a struggle for status. Many such struggles occur because, although a member has no plans at the moment, he foresees a situation in which he might need the control over the group and he therefore sets out to gain it.

He will then find himself in competition with other members in the same frame of mind. The conditions of competitiveness have been described in another chapter and they are hardly conducive to the unity of the group or its stability.

CHAPTER TWELVE

The Larger Society and Social Change

IN this last chapter we may indulge ourselves in what has been called 'the grand manner'. It is hoped to show that the approach that has proved useful for the study of the small group may be generalised in such a way as to illuminate the larger problems of sociology. We shall do this by showing how the concepts outlined previously in the book may be applied to an analysis of some elements of social change.

It is the aim of all theoretical writing to use concepts which relate to each other in a consistent manner. In doing this, one is limited by the need to check the concepts against reality and so ensure that when one abstracts phenomena for analysis, they will interrelate in the same way as the concepts. If the theory is good, the phenomena selected for study will be significant. When we assume that a good theory is one where each concept is uniquely defined by its relationship to other elements in the theory, we are compelled to assume that in the social world also each phenomenon is explained by reference to its relationship to other phenomena. The theoretical model should correspond to social reality. When elements are interrelated in such a way that a change in one element will affect, though not necessarily in equal degree, all other elements, we call the whole thus formed a system. We assume that society is a system in this sense, just as we have throughout the book discussed small group processes as systematic phenomena. Systems have certain characteristics such as size, isolation and rigidity which, as we have seen, are interesting for deductive purposes.

SOCIETY AS A SYSTEM

From the vast mass of phenomena which together constitute 'society', we are able to obtain sets of abstractions each of which

153

forms a system and each of which mirrors certain relationships in society. In this chapter we concern ourselves with three such total systems, which we shall call the value system, the social structure and the technological system. Between them these systems are exhaustive: every social phenomenon is capable of analysis in terms of them. The three systems are distinguishable in that they abstract in different ways from society. How they differ may be best shown by examples.

The technological system is the system of the material culture. It includes tools, skills, routines, methods of production and distribution of goods and services, methods of administration, transport and other such. Together they constitute the resources of the group. In the previous chapters we have referred to it as adaptive behaviour, which corresponds to the technological system at the small group level.

The social structure is composed of persons and groups in interaction; these persons and groups may differ in the extent to which they have access to resources. Therefore we must include the structural implications of decision-making—who can control or influence whom? by what means? in what circumstances? The dimension of power is located here.

The value system is the system of the collective representations of the society.[1] Besides explicit moral and religious values, it includes all other personal or cultural preferences. It determines choices between what are objectively equally useful techniques or persons, and shows itself in preferred ways of speech, preferred approaches to problems, the ranking of persons, goods, groups, aims. It determines also what needs shall be inhibited, how needs shall be expressed and satisfied, what shall be permitted as alternative patterns of living, who shall control and be controlled in specific circumstances. In the small group we have dealt with the value system in terms of the sentiments of the group, and found it to be manifested by expressive behaviour.

Each of the systems contains phenomena different in kind from those in the other two systems. Yet each affects the other. They do so in men's minds. We follow common sense in locating the systems as present, at least partially, in any man. Each man has a value system, each man perceives and operates in a large number of social relation-

[1] From Durkheim, E., *Sociology and Philosophy* (1898; tr. 1953).

154

ships, each man knows and uses a large number of the techniques at the disposal of his society.

A system may be analysed in terms of a number of relatively independent sub-systems. The elements of a sub-system may be identified as being more dependent on one another than on elements thereby defined as outside the sub-system. It would be a mistake to assume that the sub-systems are immediately recognisable as independent. Elements only remotely connected with outside elements form the nucleus of a sub-system, but the inclusion of quite a number of elements in one sub-system rather than another must depend on convenience—these elements show as much interdependence with elements in one sub-system as with those in another. On the whole, however, it may be possible to recognise natural sub-divisions.[1]

We shall be mainly concerned with sub-systems of social structure, but for other purposes it may be convenient to differentiate the technological and value systems in similar ways. The sub-systems of the social structure system we shall call groups. These groups may be very large and may themselves be capable of further sub-structuring. It is not easy to identify relatively independent groups unless one distinguishes between two kinds of interaction. There are interactions which are immediately important for the survival of the group and are recognised to be of immediate importance. In this case, only one response (or at most a very few responses) will be recognised as legitimate for each initiation of interaction and strong sanctions operate against failure to respond in the desired manner. There are, secondly, those interactions which are more remotely connected with survival, where a large variety of responses is permitted and where sanctions are milder or absent.[2]

We have noticed that status distinctions tend to come about when the problems which the environment sets the groups are very urgent. In these cases, formal channels of communication (we have tended to call them restricted channels) tend to come about.[3] Informal channels imply a freer kind of communication. Associated with the former type of interaction are power, authority and necessity as psychological bases for responding in the desired manner. The sentiment of

---

[1] See the discussion in Chapter Four, pages 51–54.
[2] The communication of information may enter into either of these types of interaction. Information may determine the behaviour of the recipient but such coercion is felt to be impersonal and is not necessarily attributed to the giver of the information.
[3] See pages 97–99 and 111.

like and dislike determines conformity in the second type of inter-action. At this point, it is as yet unnecessary to enquire whether the power is acquired or maintained by force, prestige or indispensa-bility of function. In short, persons or groups have this power in that they are thought to have, or show themselves to have, the ability to alter men's destinies. This is true in the most egalitarian as well as the most authoritarian settings.

In the social structure we identify sub-systems according to two criteria. A group may be identified as a relatively discreet unit if it is marked *internally* by a high degree of friendly interaction, and also by a certain community of norms, and *in relation to other groups* by a high degree of interaction characterised by power or necessity, by submitting to or dominating other groups, by using the other group for the satisfaction of its own needs or being so used by the other group. It will be remembered that interactions determined by neces-sity or power do not lead to greater friendliness between the two interacting units.

Groups are therefore to be distinguished from one another by a certain value of the ratio:

$$\frac{\text{friendly interaction}}{\text{enforced interaction}}$$

or perhaps

$$\frac{\text{friendly irrelevant interaction}}{\text{hostile irrelevant and task-related interaction}}$$

Two things must be noted about this. Firstly, there may be theoreti-cal difficulties in the way of finding a criterion to show whether an interaction is friendly or enforced, although it is not difficult to recognise this distinction in practice. Bound up with this is a second difficulty. The ratio has to be used to distinguish large sub-systems from one another, smaller groupings within a sub-system, and smaller groups again within these. With each further sub-structuring one may have to use different indices of friendly or enforced inter-action. At the same time, one must presumably use for each sub-structuring a different critical value of the ratio.

Groups in a society may be organised in a linear dominance-sub-mission hierarchy, from those with much power to those with little. But within this hierarchy there may be groups with equal power, which are yet distinct from one another because there are relatively few friendly, informal relations between them. The same is true within the units of an industrial organisation, between suburbs in a city, etc.

The fact that we have to distinguish between types of interaction is evidence of the impossibility of treating any system for long without reference to other systems. We shall have to show once again how the exercise of power is regulated by the value system and how the interactions which foster and are fostered by sentiment promote a characteristic idiom in which the group communicates (value system), a group-consciousness, which may hinder communication with other groups.

The fact that each of the groups has a slightly different value system emphasises their relative independence, and facilitates communication within each group. But it is the difference in the degree of power that ranks the groups in a hierarchy. It must not be assumed, however, that this implies that the social structure, and power in particular, is more fundamental than the other systems. We hope to show, rather, that the three systems reinforce one another, none being more basic than the other. Analysis, indeed, could break into this circle at any convenient point and follow it right round until the starting point itself is seen to depend on its own 'effect'.

SOCIAL CHANGE

It is useful to distinguish between two kinds of changes, namely those introduced into the system in response to changes from the outside, initially manifested through the adaptive phase in small groups, and changes through internal logic by the processes involved in latent pattern maintenance. Both these processes of change must be seen as going on concurrently. While elements in the system are being changed by impact from the outside, other elements are changing through internal logic, and because of adjustments following on previous outside impacts.

The three systems enumerated above—value, technological and social structure—are sufficiently distinct for any two of them to be regarded for certain purposes as 'outside' the third. They are all three located in the minds of men, and men may wish to keep them congruent with one another. This may produce a powerful impetus to change, for instance, if the value system countenances a dis-

157

tribution of power different from that perceived to exist in the social structure. Since all three systems develop through internal logic as well as in response to external impact, adjustments have constantly to be made to keep them congruent. Thus the changes which one system might originate in others may be inhibited or slowed down because of the inability of the other systems to absorb such a change. Current ways of thought (i.e. the current value system), for instance, may either produce or delay innovations (i.e. changes in the technological system) for which all the technical prerequisites are present in that society. In order to examine such lags and to predict the effects of changes in one system on the others, such concepts as isolation, rigidity, and congruence will need to be refined.

It is very possible that for intrinsic reasons the three systems change at different rates. Of the three, in our recent history, the technological system seems most subject to rapid change through internal logic (viz., for instance, the exponential curve of inventions).[1] The social structure and the value system seem to change rather more slowly. Much work needs to be done on these different cultural lags. If it is desired to locate the origins of change in one particular system, it may be a convenient convention always to locate it in the system that is changing most rapidly at that time.

Work on the internal rates of change of the three main systems may at present be impracticable, but useful results may be obtained where these concepts are applied to changes in small sub-systems of the social structure, such as those composed of the members of an industrial firm, a small town, or a primitive community. When such groups are relatively isolated, i.e. subject to few outside influences, it may be entirely possible to determine the rate of change inside the system in terms of three variables: the number of elements in the system, for instance, the number of persons or of families; the diameter of the system, for instance, the social distance between them (i.e. the shortest distance between the two elements that are furthest apart within the system) and the unity of the system (i.e. the total number of relationships between all the elements in the system).[2]

The path of change in a system is perhaps most easily examined by

[1] See Ogburn in Ogburn, W. F., and Nimkoff, M. T., *A Handbook of Sociology* (1947), p. 525.
[2] It is hoped to follow the present book with another in the field of sociology in which these techniques will be used for analysis.

noting the effect of an externally induced change on a system which we assume to be only slowly changing internally, as is the case, for instance, in some primitive societies. For this purpose, we have to distinguish between central and peripheral elements. Central elements are those most dependent on other elements in the system; they have many interconnections with other elements; they are so placed that in a large number of cases the peripheral elements can only affect one another via the central elements. Without introducing the notion of equilibrium, it is yet plausible to argue that a change in an element which is closely connected with other elements is subject to a reaction from those others which will minimise the effects of the change. The larger the number of interconnections, the greater will be the rectifying reaction and the more rigid the system.[1] On the other hand, a peripheral element is by definition less subject to such a corrective response. An impact from outside, directed at a central element, will therefore have less effect on the system than one aimed at a peripheral element. In a rigid system with a large number of interconnections and a relatively small difference between centre and periphery, few changes are likely to be accepted and a strong outside stimulus will either have no impact or entirely disrupt the system. In a more loosely organised system, weaker stimuli to change will have effect, and a strong stimulus will produce changes without disrupting the system.

In the social structure we have identified sub-systems or groups. In analysing change we must keep in mind not only the rigidity of a system but also the degree of isolation of the sub-systems. Rigidity is not the only danger to the survival of a group; isolation between sub-systems, or even the fragmentation of the group to isolated human beings is, as Durkheim noted, as likely to be maladaptive.[2] Many sub-systems, on the other hand, maintain elements whose function it is to communicate with other systems.[3]

Suppose we postulate two social groups relatively isolated from one another and therefore evolving mainly through internal logic. The two groups are different to start with, but they share elements in

---

[1] A system is rigid when the possibility of change is small: thus, for instance, if sub-groups in a differentiated group share the same norms and then the environment forces a change, there is no element in the group from which adaptation might come. Nothing makes sense any more. See pages 69–70 and pages 123–124.

[2] *The Division of Labour*, Book III.

[3] See pages 52–53; cf. also the Public Relation Officer.

the technological and value systems. Though they may meet much the same external pressures at much the same time, they will react to these changes in different ways, selecting different elements from outside to incorporate or reject. More and more therefore the groups will develop in different directions, will grow apart. Communication will become more and more difficult as idiosyncrasies in the value system become more pronounced. This process need not go far before the behaviour of each group becomes more or less incomprehensible to the other. In a social structure with an isolated bureaucracy, for instance, there is the danger that the bureaucrats will regard as 'things' the people outside their group, who in turn will regard the bureaucrats in terms of a formless 'they'. This unreality of the other side may lead too easily to a feeling that they are not human in quite the same way, that their needs are different and lower, and that they find their highest expression in the service of the nobler group, or of the 'good of the whole society'. As the increased isolation of the groups means that interactions of sentiment takes place largely within the groups and those for survival between the groups, the group that has power, thinking in terms of its own survival values, may tend to exploit the other group. The meaning of these new relationships may not be immediately perceived, for the value system may change rather slowly. When, however, the value system is sufficiently changed for men to be articulate about their new experience, but unable to change the system, an explosive social change may occur.

We will now examine more closely the interdependence of the three systems and how they may affect one another in social change. We have said that power ranks the groups in a hierarchy. But in a stable society, power is sanctioned by the value system which accords to each group the right and proper position which it ought to take.

This right-and-proper-place concept in its turn is related to the technological and more particularly the economic system, in that there may be a limiting factor determined by the replacement value of the group if its contribution were withdrawn. Each group possesses, besides the technological elements common to all, some elements that are peculiar to it. If one set of skills were to develop more rapidly than another, one group might contribute more to society than hitherto. This will have effects in the other two systems. When the group becomes aware of its own increased contribution, it may feel that its new importance should be recognised in terms of its rank in the social structure. Again, as elements in the technological system become more refined[1] and especially when such refinement is greater in one group than in another, it will affect the weight accorded in the value system to such elements, or to proficiency in the technological system as a whole. This will facilitate the perception that the position accorded to a group in the value system is incongruous with its actual power, and the rightness and propriety of the existing hierarchy may be questioned. It depends, however, on the value system whether contribution in the technological system is regarded as a just criterion of rank in the social structure system. But the value system is itself susceptible to change, though changes in it may be slow.

In a stable society, the existing social structure and value system will tend to be seen as obviously the just ones. If, however, there are rapid changes in one system, this will produce instability in a society. In our example, rapid technological change came most aptly to the mind. Had we started at a different point in our analysis, however, cause and effect would have been seen as differently distributed between the systems.

Our final illustration, an analysis of one element of change in our own society, compels us for a moment to move again to the psychological level. All three systems originate, and the value system formulates, needs which must be satisfied. According to one political value system, the democratic-welfare one, one group is split off and given power on the understanding that the emergent needs of those who gave the power are satisfied. In a democratic country with a multi-party system, the wishes of the voters have to be correctly interpreted if the party is to remain in power. As these wishes may be incompatible, and are in any case liable to change whenever action is taken, constant reinterpretation is needed. The competing interests of the parties—they both want power—makes it expedient for them to make constant readjustments in the social structure and value systems. On the one hand, they formulate the criteria according to which power and other rewards should be distributed in the society in response to changes in social structure; on the other hand, they

---

[1] By refined, we mean that it is structured so minutely that small distinctions can be drawn, so that one may know in what ways various elements relate together.

make the changes which will bring the social structure nearer to the ideal advocated in their value system. They are induced to maintain the *status quo* or to make changes because their power depends on the extent to which they can gratify the needs which they themselves may have evoked.

By associating the groups that have great power—the competing political parties—with each other and by associating them with the group of voters, modes of communication are institutionalised which ensure that the groups shall not grow irreparably apart. One of the functions of these groups is therefore to facilitate communication between the systems. By this constant process of interpretation and reinterpretation the time lag between changes in one system and the others is shortened and discrepancies between the systems are brought out and may be corrected.

A Study of Relationships in three small Groups

AN English teacher of social psychology is handicapped compared with an American one when it comes to experimental
work. There must be many of us who have read with envy of
the large American classes which can be split up into sixty groups of
four or forty groups of six members and for whom the acquisition of
credits is an incentive for submitting to the indignity of being a
guinea-pig. With such resources precise experimental work is
possible. The study of which a short account is given here is not up
to that standard. The findings must all be taken with a careful
scepticism because of the small number of subjects involved.

I take this opportunity to thank the students who made this study
possible.

METHOD

Two groups of six and one group of seven young men met weekly
for ten weeks. They were composed of first-year University students,
who had volunteered to take part in this study. The groups were
matched as far as possible for age, service experience, and course of
study taken at the University. No selection according to tempera-
ment or personality was possible, but one criterion was kept in
mind: that members should not be over-anxious under observation.
The members were so selected that those coming to the same group
were unlikely to meet between experimental sessions. Matters of
common interest were discussed for about an hour at a time, after
which the subjects completed a questionnaire. There was no restriction on the topic; any member could change the subject any time he
wished and this was expressly stated by the experimenter.

The method of observation was very simple. The members sat in a

163

small room, in a rough circle, with the observer just outside the circle.

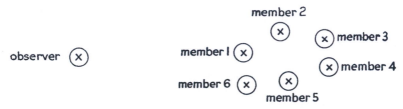

The observer recorded the interaction in the group by noting down the number by which the member who was speaking was identified. The observation sheet thus consisted of a long series of numbers between 1 and 6. Each speech was called a 'contribution' to the interaction process, or a 'communication'. In this way one obtained the sequence and the frequency of contributions made by the members at each meeting.

The unit of verbal interaction is quite clearly the word directed by one person to another. It is here assumed that this is a willed act, i.e. that Jack spoke to Bill because he wanted to. There are elements of doubt about this assumption, (i) because Jack may have wanted to express an opinion and have turned to Bill rather than Tom for reasons unconnected with either, and (ii) because Tom may have 'caught' a remark and by answering it have caused it to be observed as directed to him in spite of Jack's intention.

Neither of these considerations can affect the basic assumption seriously because normal directed remarks occur so much more frequently than these chance events. The speaker and the person who answers him are therefore taken to be the significant elements in the interaction process.

The direction of a remark is important regardless of the purpose or motive of its content, that is to say, regardless of whether it supports or attacks the person to whom it is made. The important aspect is that interaction has been initiated, just as in dominance-submission studies it is a prior consideration which child gets its way with the others and a secondary one whether he or the others benefit most by his action. It must also be remembered that it is difficult to keep going a conversation in which all are of the same mind, and the members of these groups felt, rightly or wrongly, that they were there to talk. That being so, Jack, when he wishes to make contact with Bill, will be as likely to react to Bill's contribution to the conversation with dissent or interrogation as with support.

Moreover, there is a sense in which members speak by permission of one another. They could be prevented from speaking by being simply overshouted; in fact, this sometimes happened. The simple frequency with which a member speaks means that his group expects him to speak this often and neither more nor less. One may feel justified, therefore, in the assumption that interaction on the verbal level is a meaningful concept, in some ways related to the particular composition of the group and the desire for contacts among its members.

THE NUMBER OF CONTRIBUTIONS MADE BY MEMBERS OF THE GROUP

A man's personality shows not only in what he says but also in the freedom with which he speaks. Since personality is relatively stable, one might expect the number of communications made by a member of a particular group to be stable also. Moreover, since people differ in personality one would expect them to differ characteristically in the degree to which they take part in conversation. Table I (app.) shows by percentage the share each member had in the total amount of communication.

Table I

PERCENTAGE OF THE TOTAL NUMBER OF COMMUNICATIONS
FOR EACH MEMBER OF THREE GROUPS

Group A. Number of meetings

Member	1	2	3	4	5	6	7	8	9	10
1	17	23	23	17	13	21	22	21	12	—
2	24	19	12	17	13	12	12	14	19	—
3	21	20	17	18	19	16	18	16	15	—
4	17	—	12	18	19	17	14	17	18	—
5	9	18	17	16	19	14	14	12	10	—
6	11	21	19	17	17	20	20	20	26	—
Totals	99	101	100	100	100	100	100	100	100	—

Group B.   Number of Meetings

Member	1	2	3	4	5	6	7	8	·9	10
1	12	11	10	14	16	14	5	11	6	10
2	17	24	15	29	17	21	19	17	20	21
3	7	9	6	7	9	9	5	12	15	10
4	18	—	16	—	17	16	23	15	22	23
5	19	26	20	19	20	16	19	18	13	12
6	26	29	33	32	21	25	30	26	24	23
Totals	99	99	100	100	100	101	101	99	100	99

Group C.   Number of meetings

Member	1	2	3	4	5	6	7	8	9	10
1	25	28	26	29	20	27	26	—	37	25
2	14	20	26	25	17	15	26	—	21	25
3	13	17	10	12	18	23	13	—	13	15
4	3	2	0	0	2	0	0	—	0	1
5	2	4	7	1	11	7	4	—	1	5
6	7	4	3	4	4	0	0	—	0	2
7	36	26	28	29	27	27	31	—	28	27
Totals	100	101	100	100	99	99	100	—	100	100

It will be seen that there is a definite regularity in the amount that each member contributes relative to other members throughout the ten meetings. He does not speak twice as much at one meeting as he does at another. This regularity is the more remarkable in that all have an equal chance of contributing to the topic in hand or of changing the topic to one more congenial to them.

One word of reservation is needed. Communications may vary not only in number, but in length. In the groups reported here, the observer could only record the former of these dimensions so that a mere grunt of assent carries as much weight in our statistics as does a three-minute speech. This means that certain regularities of behaviour of which the observer is convinced are to some extent masked.

One of these regularities is that some members of the group speak frequently but briefly, while others make fewer but more lengthy contributions. Moreover, it seems as though each member has in mind a standard time which he feels entitled to fill, so that when he feels he has spoken too much, or too little, in the first half-hour of the meeting, he will modify his volubility during the second half in order to average on the whole his self-appointed allowance of communication. Finally, it seems as though the amount of activity which each member allows himself tends to approximate more nearly to the group norm as time goes on.

THE IDENTIFICATION OF SUB-GROUPS

When members of loosely organised groups such as the ones under observation in this study are free to speak, when and to whom they like, they come to speak more frequently to some than to others. Conversation is rarely general; more usually it is in the hands of a few who hand over their verbal dominance to another few who are in their turn superseded. In this way there is always a minority interacting while the others are passive. More technically, the small group consists of smaller sub-groups, the whole being kept together because each person is a member of several sub-groups.

We must now consider methods for identifying these sub-groups. Since the study was concerned with verbal behaviour only, one could use a very simple method of recording, taking into account only the order in which members spoke. A sub-group is defined as a group whose members speak more frequently with each other than with those outside that sub-group. Groups were isolated on the following principle.

From a list of contributions such as:

$$6\ 3\ 4\ 3\ 5\ 4\ 5\ 3\ 2\ 4\ 3\ 5\ 6\ 5\ 6\ 5\ 4\ 5\ \text{etc. etc.},$$

where each number stands for a member of the experimental group, one takes the first three as a sub-group, i.e. 6–3–4, then, dropping the first of these and adding the next, one obtains another sub-group 3–4–3, and so 4–3–5, 3–5–4, 5–4–5, etc. No distinction is made between sub-groups consisting of the same members in a different order, i.e. 4–3–5 and 3–5–4, because it was felt that the method was too crude to allow of valid interpretation of such refinement. Again, no distinction is drawn between 3–4–3 and 4–3–4; groups like these are called pairs because only two members are involved. The experimenter checked up on one session and found that if these two forms of a pair are counted separately there is little difference in the frequency with which either occurs. One might venture the hypothesis, however, that if a group of the 1–2–1 type

167

occurs significantly more frequently than one of the 2–1–2 type, member 1 will be the more dominant member of the pair.

For this definition of a sub-group to have any meaning, it must be established that these sub-groupings are not thrown up by chance. This was our first problem. If Jack and Bill talk three times as often as Tom and Harry, then the former two are much more likely to occur in sequence with one another and even with Tom and with Harry, than Tom and Harry with one another. In this way the significance of the groupings formed by the less expressive members would be masked. A model had therefore to be constructed to give the frequencies with which one would expect each grouping to occur on the basis of the number of contributions only, i.e. if no one directed more remarks to those members whom he preferred than to those to whom he was indifferent.[1] The actual frequencies would either correspond to this expected frequency, or be higher, or lower. These differences were standardised by finding:

$$\frac{\text{actual frequency}}{\text{expected frequency}}$$

If the result is greater than unity, the sub-group in question appears more frequently than could be expected from chance alone; if the result is a fraction of one (1) the sub-group occurs less frequently than can be accounted for by chance.

In this connection one may mention a to some extent analogous argument put forward in sociometry. A social group is distinguished from a collection of individuals by the criterion that in the former the number of mutual choices is well above chance level. In other words, a social group must be structured in such a way that smaller groups stand out with some permanence against an undifferentiated social background.

This method of analysis clearly has disadvantages. Spurious sub-groups are likely to be counted in. For example, since the content of communication was not noted there was no way of knowing when a new topic of conversation was introduced. If Tom then introduces a subject after Jack and Bill have been talking about something else, and if he addresses himself mainly to Harry, yet sub-groups Jack–Bill–Tom and Bill–Tom–Harry will be counted in observation. However, such groups would appear much less fre-

[1] See Note (a) at end of Appendix.

quently than genuine ones, though the latter will be masked by them to some extent.

Another difficulty arises from the fact that the length of the speeches was not recorded. If one could have weighted the contributions according to their length, this would to some extent have proved a corrective, and the structure would have appeared more clearly.

Of all the social contacts, the easiest to initiate and to maintain is a pair. Here each member has to take into account only the personality requirements of one other, whereas in a trio each has to integrate the two contacts desired one with the other as well as with the self. Also, question and answer is the simplest form of conversation and tends to give an impression of such ease that it may discourage a third party from seeking to enter the group. It is not surprising, therefore, that a very great number of groups consisted of pairs.

To obtain an index the actual number of pairs was calculated in proportion to the expected number, i.e.

$$\frac{\text{actual frequency of pair groups (or trios)}}{\text{expected frequency of pair groups (or trios)}}$$

Table II (app.) shows the data and the results.

It will be seen that the number of pair groups is considerably greater than can be accounted for by chance. The average over the whole series of meetings for the ratio actual : expected frequency of pairs is 1·9 for Group A; 1·7 for Group B; and 1·5 for Group C. Trios on the other hand occur less frequently than could have been expected. The average of ratios for trios is 0·75 for Group A; 0·76 for Group B; and also 0·76 for Group C.

Next we must examine the relative frequencies with which particular sub-groups of members formed and persisted throughout the series of meetings. For each sub-group the ratio actual : expected frequency was calculated; each sub-group was then classified each week into one of the following classes:

top quartile   (most frequently occurring sub-groups)
bottom quartile (least frequently occurring sub-groups)
middle two quartiles.

The aim of this analysis was to show that the communication pat-

169

Table II

ACTUAL AND CALCULATED FREQUENCIES OF PAIRS AND TRIOS WITH THE RATIO

$$\frac{\text{actual frequency}}{\text{expected frequency}} \text{ for pairs and trios.}$$

	weeks									
	1	2	3	4	5	6	7	8	9	10
Group A.										
pairs										
actual	213	296	320	293	339	302	271	219	310	—
expected	87	161	190	167	167	163	166	112	169	—
trios										
actual	192	309	557	543	457	484	523	301	442	—
expected	318	447	687	658	640	624	628	410	587	—
ratio of actual to expected										
pairs	2·4	1·8	1·7	1·8	2·1	1·9	1·6	2·0	1·8	—
trios	0·60	0·69	0·81	0·83	0·71	0·78	0·83	0·73	0·75	—
Group B.										
pairs										
actual	279	292	282	324	277	277	352	225	284	214
expected	139	179	164	208	154	164	181	129	152	150

trios actual	326	320	331	332	442	464	339	346	381	418
trios expected	465	427	449	449	566	579	509	440	512	483
ratio of actual to expected — pairs	2·0	1·6	1·7	1·6	1·8	1·7	1·9	1·7	1·9	1·4
ratio of actual to expected — trios	0·70	0·75	0·74	0·74	0·78	0·80	0·67	0·79	0·74	0·87

Group C.

pairs actual	—	247	311	278	332	271	269	—	332	257
pairs expected	—	140	209	192	183	166	186	—	246	154
trios actual	—	276	390	323	442	307	279	—	303	299
trios expected	—	380	489	414	599	398	357	—	412	393
ratio of actual to expected — pairs	—	1·8	1·5	1·4	1·8	1·6	1·4	—	1·4	1·7
ratio of actual to expected — trios	—	0·73	0·80	0·78	0·74	0·77	0·78	—	0·74	0·76

171

terns form a structure—a system of interrelated sub-groups—which to be meaningful units of analysis must have some stability over time and are not unique patterns for each encounter. This does not mean, of course, that the pattern must necessarily be repeated in its exact form at each meeting. New emerging sub-groups only gradually rise into the top quartile; other sub-groups may start in the highest quartile and gradually disappear.

Since a group of six members can be split into fifteen possible pairs and twenty possible trios, the quartile tables are not given in detail. A short summary is given instead, founded on the following basis. At the simplest level, evidence of a stable and therefore systematic structure of communication sub-groups is found when over the series of meetings:

1. Certain sub-groups occur regularly in the top quartile.
2. Certain sub-groups occur regularly in the lowest quartile.
3. Still other sub-groups never occur in either quartile.

Where a structure of communication sub-groups is non-systematic there are many sub-groups which occur at one time at the top end of the frequency distribution, at other times near the bottom, and then perhaps at the top again. But where a sub-group changes in a consistent way from a phase in which it appears frequently to one in which it does not appear, or *vice versa*, this may be called a regular change: it does not falsify the hypothesis that there is a systematic structure. Not all changes are random variations. For the analysis three categories are used:

(i) *stable sub-groups* containing the cases corresponding to 1, 2, 3 above;
(ii) *changing sub-groups* containing the cases which change in a regular manner from more frequent to less, or *vice versa*;
(iii) *unstable sub-groups* containing the cases which appear in random fashion.

To the extent to which there are more cases in the first two categories than in the last, the hypothesis of a system of communication sub-groups is proven. Tables III (app.) and IV (app.) show that the hypothesis is justified by the data.

Table III

THE NUMBER AND PERCENTAGE OF STABLE, CHANGING AND UNSTABLE
TRIOS IN THE THREE GROUPS

Group	stable no.	%	changing no.	%	unstable no.	%	total no.	%
A	10	50	4	20	6	30	20	100
B	8	40	5	25	7	35	20	100
C	20	57	6	17	9	26	35	99

Table IV

THE NUMBER AND PERCENTAGE OF STABLE, CHANGING AND UNSTABLE
PAIRS IN THE THREE GROUPS

Group	stable no.	%	changing no.	%	unstable no.	%	total no.	%
A	6	40	5	33	4	27	15	100
B	9	60	3	20	3	20	15	100
C	14	66	3	15	4	19	21	100

POPULARITY AND VOLUBILITY

The impression one gains of the personality of other members of
a group depends on the way that person acts, expresses himself. In
the present case, conversation was the only activity, that is, the only
means of expression. It is common sense that the quantity of activity
(even of directed activity—interaction) will not in itself establish a
man's popularity. Selfish talkers who monopolise the conversation
are not generally popular, while other prolific talkers may have
something to say which the group wants to hear and thus become
popular. But although the amount of activity cannot be the only
determinant of the degree of positive sentiment attracted, there is in
this study a good correlation. Compare the following two lists:

Most popular members:
  Group A, 1, 2, 4; Group B, 2, 4, 6; Group C, 2, 3, 7.
Most voluble members:
  Group A, 1, 3, 6; Group B, 2, 4, 5, 6; Group C, 1, 2, 7.
Six members occur in both lists.

At the other end of the scale, if a member of the group fails to

173

THE STUDY OF GROUPS

speak at all, the other members lose interest in him and, having no way of judging him, rank him last. This extreme case is presented by member C4 who finally never said a word and never came to be chosen first or second by anyone for anything.

It would appear, therefore, that members of a group need some information before they make up their minds on whom they like. Where this information is not forthcoming, as when a member takes no part in interaction and thus gives no evidence of what he is like, the other members ignore him. At the beginning of a series of meetings at least, information of this kind is of the highest importance. Anyone prepared to supply it is better liked, at this early stage apparently regardless of whether the information he supplies makes him out to be a pleasant companion or not. It will be shown later that in Group A, where members tended to be very similar in the amount they spoke, the members were just beginning to pay attention to the content of what was being said when the series came to an end, and to judge on the basis of that the suitability of different members as associates for different activities.

THE EVOLUTION OF SENTIMENT

Wherever people meet together regularly over a period of time, emotional ties, either positive or negative, come to be formed. In this section we will analyse the development of these ties by means of a study of the popularity scores of the members. It was a methodological necessity to ask a good number of questions so that the response of one week would not be remembered the next, as this might influence members to be more consistent than they might otherwise have been in their sentiment structures. The fact that we had in any case to ask a number of sociometric questions, instead of the customary one or two, induced us to investigate as a side-issue the relations between structures formed on the basis of psyche-criteria and those based on sociocriteria.

To select the questions for our questionnaire a crude adaptation of Thurstone's attitude statement selection procedure was used. From fifteen cards bearing statements which contribute toward the definition of 'a friend', a number of students were asked to separate those that related more to association based on common interests, from those that related more to association for the performance of work. Out of 26 students, 24 grouped together questions 1, 3 and 6

174

of the questionnaire below, and 19 of these 24 distinguished between these questions, which were psychecriteria, and questions 2, 4 and 5, which were sociocriteria.

The finished questionnaire looked as below:

In the following questions you are required to range other members of your group according to first choice, second choice, third choice, and so on till last choice. Please do not leave anyone out. Check up that there are 5 (6) names in each space. It does not matter if two lists are the same.

1. If you found you had left your money at home, from whom would you borrow for the day?
2. Who do you think would be a valuable member on any committee?
3. If you had a spare ticket for a concert, to whom would you offer it first?
4. Different people know different sets of facts; whose total knowledge would you most like to have?
5. If you could read only twenty books for the rest of your life, whom would you prefer to select them for you?
6. If you had to share rooms with someone, whom would you choose?

In sociometry it is often stressed that sociometric questions must always refer to an actual situation which can be brought about as a result of the answers to the questions. The reason given is that the choices will then be made on a reality level. But if one had used the answers to a question to modify the situation in this study, one would have defeated one's own ends. Officially formed groups on a permanent basis develop in-group feelings and the early expressed preferences are thus confirmed. When one wants the situation to retain its unstructured character there must be no reality testing. The subjects did not have to act on their expressed preferences and they were thus left free to change their minds. The questions used could easily be translated into everyday experience. The amount of empathy needed for the subject to feel himself into the situation was very small. Since the results are consistent with one another and with a theory, they obviously refer to something, and it is difficult to see what they could refer to apart from liking.

It is, moreover, doubtful whether it is altogether fair to distinguish

175

between realistic and phantasy choices in the manner of socio-metry. The popularity of the football captain, and in fact the whole sociodynamic effect, and by definition any unreciprocated choice implies that reality conditions have for the moment been ignored by the chooser. Such choices always represent the chooser's aspirations to some extent and confuse the group of which he would like to be a member with the group of which he is likely to be a member. If I could choose Socrates to be my neighbour at dinner I would do so. I am therefore bound to put him down first on my sociometric list. But I know that Socrates might prefer many others to sit beside him before he chose me. I therefore introduce a reality factor into my choices. I much prefer Socrates to Phaedrus but I know that when it comes to the point I shall have much more chance of sitting by Phaedrus than by Socrates. I can therefore either put Socrates first, knowing I haven't a hope of sitting beside him, thus offending against the reality-principle, or I can put Phaedrus first lest worst befall, but in spite of my preference.

Each week the members of the group ranked each other in order of preference for association in the six activities presented in the questionnaire. If one adds the rankings each person received each week from his fellow members this would give a general index of that person's popularity.

Thus in the first week member A1 is put first on five criteria and second on a sixth criterion by member A2 and by member A3. Member A4 puts him first once, third twice, and fourth three times. Member A5 puts him fourth three times and fifth three times. Member A6 puts him first once, second once, third twice and fourth once and fifth once.

Group A, Member 1

criterion	1	2	3	4	5	6
from member	23456	23456	23456	23456	23456	23456
week one	21443	11443	11145	11452	12351	11345

Adding his scores for week one, from all members on all criteria, we arrive at A1's popularity score which is 73. This score can be compared to that of other members in the same week, or to his own score in subsequent weeks. The results cannot be of much interest in themselves since as one person becomes more popular and is there-

176

fore ranked more highly, another must necessarily take a lower rank and become 'less popular'.

More important to a study of group sentiments is an investigation into the generality with which a member's popularity is established; that is to say, an investigation into the range within which opinion about a person's popularity varied. For this purpose each member's popularity score was averaged each week. A1's total score, for instance, was 73 in the first week; his average that week was 1.2. (The scale runs from one to six, with one–high and six–low.) The deviation round this mean, disregarding signs, is obviously an indication of the degree of disagreement about a person's popularity that exists in the group. If the sum of deviation is small, agreement on a member's popularity is large. Table IV (app.) gives the sum of absolute deviations for all members' evaluations of one another each week. The greater this sum, the more disagreement exists in the group on the popularity ranking of the members.

Table V

THE SUM OF ABSOLUTE DEVIATIONS ROUND THE MEAN OF MEMBERS'
EVALUATION OF ONE ANOTHER

(Six criteria)

Week	Group A	Group B	Group C		Total
			actual	scaled[1]	
1	157	262	297	212	531
2	175	197	283	202	574
3	153	189	254	181	525
4	182	168	256	183	533
5	149	171	232	301	521
6	163	144	220	157	464
7	137	161	233	131	497
8	139	159	241	172	470
9	136	158	251	179	473

[1] The actual sum of absolute deviations was multiplied by six-sevenths in order to be able to compare group C which contains seven members, with groups A and B, which contains six members each.

THE SUM OF ABSOLUTE DEVIATIONS AS ABOVE FOR MEMBERS WHOSE
POPULARITY DECREASES

Week	Group A	Group B	Group C	
			actual	scaled[1]
1	60	38	98	70
2	53	56	109	78
3	54	46	80	57
4	57	41	75	54
5	53	46	85	61
6	65	62	76	54
7	43	39	88	59
8	50	50	74	52
9	50	47	83	53
10	—	43	77	55

THE SUM OF ABSOLUTE DEVIATIONS AS ABOVE FOR MEMBERS WHOSE
POPULARITY INCREASES

Week	Group A	Group B	Group C	
			actual	scaled[1]
1	66	41	71	51
2	44	—	66	47
3	70	52	56	40
4	69	—	62	44
5	66	40	70	50
6	59	45	67	42
7	53	30	62	44
8	55	26	57	41
9	49	36	55	39
10	—	39	67	48

Unless one can show that the popularity assessments each week
are related to one another in some way, one has no means of knowing whether one is dealing with a phenomenon which has a psychological reality in the minds of the experimental subjects. As before,
one must seek for changes or uniformities from week to week to
reveal that one is not dealing with random figures. Suppose, for
instance, one were to find an increasing agreement within the group
of each member's popularity and specific merits. This would indicate

[1] The actual sum of absolute deviations was multiplied by six-sevenths in order to
be able to compare group C which contains seven members, with groups A and B,
which contains six members each.

that the assessments related to a factor which had meaning for the members and that they had the same meaning for all of them. The growing agreement in the group on the popularity status of each member would show in the fact that the sum of deviations from the mean of all members' ranking of each other diminish as the series of meetings continues. This can be tested by a coefficient of disarray.[1] These coefficients for our groups are: for Group A – 0·56 (significance level 0·02), for Group B – 0·78 (significance level 0·001) and for Group C – 0·44 (significance level 0·06). This growing agreement is not specific to either likes or dislikes. If one takes separately the three highest and the three lowest rankings in a group each week, the same trend toward diminishing sums of deviations is discernible, though at a lower level of significance.

This is a remarkable result. It must be remembered that members had no opportunity to meet outside the experimental situation to gossip about the personality of fellow members. Nor did they do so under observation. Yet a group norm was arrived at and increasingly conformed to.

SOCIOGROUPS AND PSYCHEGROUPS

In sociometric theory a sociogroup is based on preferences involving work in the group, such as co-operation in a common task. The psychegroup is based on purely personal preferences such as, for instance, association in leisure time. When questions relating to both kinds of criteria are presented to the subject at the same time, the sentiment structures resulting from these two kinds of criteria tend to differ in many ways.[2] When only one criterion has been presented to the subject he will almost invariably treat it as a psychecriterion: that is to say, if you cannot choose your friends for a picnic you will choose them for your football team regardless of their skill as footballers. It must be noted that most of the data concerning this had been obtained in circumstances where meetings between persons were externally controlled, as they were, for instance, in the girls' reformatory where Jennings did her work.

Three of the questions in the questionnaire used in the study described above involved psychegroup relationships (questions 1, 3

[1] See Note (b) at end of Appendix.
[2] Jennings, H. H., *Leadership and Isolation* (second edition), Longmans, Green, New York, 1950; 'Sociometric Differentiation of the Psychegroup and the Sociogroup', *Sociometry*, X, 1947.

and 6) and three involved sociogroup relationships (questions 2, 4 and 5). One would therefore expect members of the experimental groups to distinguish between these two kinds of question in much the same way that the subjects in the preliminary testing had done. They did not do so. There is no real difference between rankings for criteria 1, 3, 6 and rankings according to criteria 2, 4, 6. One must therefore conclude that whatever psychological function was expressed by the rankings of the members, it was not one that distinguished between psycherelationships and sociorelationships, however valid that distinction might have seemed intellectually.

It is worth noting in passing that Gibb,[1] too, found that there was 'considerable overlap' between his sociogroups and psychegroups. As in the present study, his subjects were presented with more than two questions.

One is inclined to take these results at their face-value. The distinction commonly drawn in sociometry between these kinds of groups needs much qualification. One doubt we have already expressed: that persons free to choose their associates may not need to distinguish so rigidly as those whose interactions are controlled by an authority. But may not the whole difference between the two kinds of structure be no more than an experimental artefact? One obtains a sociogram by asking the subject to name the person with whom he wants to associate. Such a sociogram will differ from either of the ones obtained by asking a 'psyche' question and a 'socio' question on one occasion. Sociometric theory has held that these two are refinements of the former, i.e. 'pure types' of the former confused response. But it may equally well be that the first response was indicative of a genuine but general desire for association, which *could not* be split again into two different feelings.

The insistence of the sociometrist that the two kinds of criterion must be presented simultaneously now begins to sound suspicious. The two questions together begged a third. If I have to name a friend to work with and a friend with whom to spend my leisure time I tend to interpret these instructions so that I name one friend for work and *another* for play. There is a pressure implicit in the phrasing which induces one to name two persons rather than one. The very fact of asking two questions produces, according to our argument, two different responses.

[1] Gibb, C. A., 'The Sociometry of Leadership', *Sociometry*, VIII, 1950.

Moreno[1] himself found that mentally retarded children did not distinguish so readily between the two kinds of groups. The explanation tentatively presented here is that this was due to the fact that the subtle distinction implied in asking the two questions simultaneously was lost to them. They did not feel called upon to differentiate in the answers because to them there was no difference between the questions. The mentally adequate person is impressed by the theoretical distinction although in fact emotionally there is often no conflict between the kinds of association. In the present study, and in Gibb's study, there were several questions all jumbled together; thus one approximates more closely to the situation of a single 'who is your friend' kind of question than if two questions were asked. As a result, a single permanent structure not divisible into sociogroups and psychegroups was obtained.

There is some evidence which is very tentative and needs to be tested further, that subjects do use a multiple-question sociometric questionnaire in a systematic way. It seems that our subjects used the six questions at first as a unified whole, in fact as a single question might be used, in order to rank their fellow members in a general order of preference. A man they like will be ranked first on all the six criteria; one they dislike will be ranked last on all the criteria. This stage is short in conditions where it is easy for members to perceive one another's personality, i.e. where members are able to express themselves at length in the conversation. In our study these conditions held in the groups where all members spoke roughly the same as the others and where they all tended to speak a good deal. In this way they come to know one another.

As the group members become more familiar with one another, a second phase sets in. As sufficient information about each member accumulates, it becomes possible to recognise the personal characteristics of each member in more detail. It comes to be recognised that one member might be a better associate for a particular activity and he is therefore ranked first on the appropriate criterion. Another member might be more fun for another activity and he will be ranked first on another criterion. Whereas at first, therefore, the order of preferences listed by any member is the same for any criterion, they tend to become less similar as the meetings continue. This process is greatly delayed and not so clearly observable in the group where all

[1] Moreno, J. L., *Who Shall Survive?*, Beacon House, Beacon, New York, 1934.

members tended to speak much less and where there were great inequalities in the frequency with which various members spoke.

Possibly one could translate this into sociometric terminology and say that where there are many criteria available the individual uses them to make clear to himself which members are eligible for his psychegroup. While he is preoccupied with this he cannot give his mind to deciding for which activity he would prefer to associate with particular members.

What seems to happen, therefore, is that both psyche-criteria and socio-criteria are used first of all to help the group member make up his mind which people he prefers to others. Whatever the questions are, they are used to decide what the psychegroup is. When this has been established with a fair measure of security, *all* the questions take on a more sociogroup significance. In accordance with simple psychological laws, the meaning of a stimulus, in this case a question, changes according to the context in which a subject finds himself. His perception of the questions changes as his perception of the group becomes more structured. When the structure of his knowledge about other members of the group is relatively undifferentiated, there is no way in which he can discriminate between six very similar stimuli. When his perception does become refined, he can discriminate between them all. But at no time does his perception allow him to distinguish between sociocriteria and psychecriteria and in no other way.

BION: THE BASIC ASSUMPTIONS OF THE GROUP

Our observation techniques enabled us to test certain hypotheses which W. R. Bion (1948–50) constructed on the basis of his work with psychotherapeutic groups. According to Bion, there are two different kinds of groups. One is the *work or sophisticated group*, which is composed of members with rational personalities who wish to keep their procedure and their purpose rational. They do this for fear that the *group mentality* of members, which disregards individual welfare and is concerned only with the group as such, should gain the upper hand. All group members contribute to this mentality and are unconscious of doing so.

Members preoccupied with the group mentality can see the purpose of the group only in terms of certain basic assumptions. There are three of these basic assumptions. They may manifest themselves

· 182

either in *pairing groups,* whose purpose is sexual, or in *dependence groups* in which an outside agency (who may in other ways be a group member) is supposed to be helpful and protective as regards the group purpose, or the group may take to *flight or fight.*

When the group is not on a sophisticated level it is always acting on one of these basic assumptions. It may act on a particular basic assumption for several sessions or there may be many rapid alternations within an hour. The more rapid the alternations, the more dangerous, according to Bion, the situation becomes. Bion's terminology has obvious structural implications, an examination of which will prove most fruitful.

When one looks at the interaction processes in the groups described in this Appendix one finds, especially at the beginning of the series, such communication sequences as 1 2 1 3 1 2 1 6 1 4 . . . 1 6 2 6 4 6 3 6 5 6. It does not seem fanciful to say that these must be the structural counterparts of the basic assumption of dependence in Bion's groups, with 1 and later 6 cast by the group as the leader on whom they are dependent for help and protection against the evil of embarrassing silence. Silence was regarded as an evil by the members of the groups because they knew that the research worker was interested in their conversation and therefore they felt they ought to speak as much as possible. They therefore fed questions and encouragement to the leader, who fulfilled his function as long as he could, but, becoming exhausted, finally ceased to respond. Moreover, group members could not but perceive that conversation was not very general, and was not becoming general either, and they interpreted this to mean that their leader was not doing his job properly. For both these reasons they would then try their luck with another member of the group and the whole sequence would repeat itself. The first meeting in all the groups consisted almost entirely of such sequences punctuated by fairly long silences, which were presumably the structural counterpart of the 'flight' basic assumption. Silence was the only means of flight short of not turning up at the meeting.

After this stage, interaction patterns changed to correspond more to the sequence type 6 1 6 1 6 1 6 1 6 1 2 4 2 4 2 4 2 4. Here the pairing basic assumption has come uppermost. It seemed to the observer that the satisfaction which the group as a whole gained from this phase was not purely derived from the pairing assumption,

183

though this might be the satisfaction gained by the two actually in communication. The rest of the group, however, having now completely abdicated all its function to the leadership—which in these cases consisted of two persons—was still in the dependence situation. The group as a whole did not even have to do the feeding and encouraging of the leader which was necessary in the pure dependence group. As long as conversation was kept up, which is easy in a two-sided conversation, interaction was going on and it was this which was perceived by the group to be the purpose for which the research worker had called the group together.

It is not so easy to fit the 'flight or fight' basic assumption with a structural counterpart. Flight can, of course, be accounted for by silence, but with the method of analysis used fight cannot be distinguished from work.

It is interesting to note that these phases were clearly distinguishable. Though they alternated, the alternations were not as rapid as those of Bion's groups seem to have been. Moreover, they seem to have been in three main stages. This difference from Bion's findings can easily be accounted for. When one considers that the first stage was one of dependence on a leader, the second of the pairing kind and the third the sophisticated work kind, it becomes possible to see these processes as ones in which the members come gradually to feel more secure. This condition cannot have been so easily attained by a group of neurotics unwilling to be cured and under Bion's forceful care.

Our use of Bion also throws some light on the decline of pair communication groups. Both dependence groups (1 2 1 3 1 4 1 5) and pairing groups (2 3 2 3 2 3) are obviously counted in terms of pair communication groups. In the latter stages of the series of meetings work may have become the purpose of the meeting and larger structures may be more suitable for this. The groups were undoubtedly 'sophisticated' in Bion's sense later in the series. The totals of the number of communications show in all groups a peculiar rise and fall during the series of meetings, rising from about 400 at the beginning to about 750 at the sixth meeting and declining to about 650 at the tenth meeting. These changes may be attributed to the larger 'flight' element present at the outset of the series, which would obviously reduce the number of communications made. The middle stage could be accounted for partly by a growing work purpose (this

184

would bring it to about 650) and the surplus explained in terms of a reaction formation to flight or silence, about which the members felt guilty. There would be at this stage a large number of short communications calculated to fill in any gap of silence which might occur. This reaction would eventually wear off and the group settle down to the total characteristic of the last stage. The observer believes that if it had been possible to allow for the length of communication as well as for frequency, the totals of the second and third stages would be roughly the same—i.e. the proportion of silence to speech would be the same—but the hour would in the one case be filled by many small communications, in the other by slightly longer ones, but fewer of them.

As group members came to be more accustomed to the set-up they came to feel more secure. Whenever there was for some reason an increase in insecurity, there was a regression to a basic assumption. When, for instance, C1 was absent from the eighth meeting of Group C, the whole group took refuge in flight or silence. The number of communications dropped to half; two members never opened their mouth in that meeting or the next; there were terrible, long silences. At the ninth meeting C1 came back and was immediately very strongly re-established in his position as a leader, more strongly than ever before. As a rule C1 accounted for about a quarter of the total number of communications made, but on this occasion he came close to 40 per cent.

A great deal of work still remains to be done on the connection of structure and sentiment.

APPENDIX. NOTE (a)

THE COMPUTATION OF EXPECTED VALUES

Let N = number of contributions made in an hour.

F_r = frequency with which r speaks out of the total number of contributions made in an hour.

P_r = the probability that r shall speak next.

Then $P_r = \dfrac{F_r}{N}$

$G_r = N - F_r$

Pairs. The probability that *s* shall speak after *r*.

$$P_{r,s,r} = P_r \frac{P_s}{1-P_r} \cdot \frac{P_r}{1-P_s}$$

$$P_{s,r,s} = P_s \frac{P_r}{1-P_s} \cdot \frac{P_s}{1-P_r}$$

Then the probability that *r* and *s* will form a group either *r, s, r* or *s, r, s*.

$$P_{rs} = \frac{P_r}{1-P_s} \cdot \frac{P_s}{1-P_r} \cdot (P_r + P_s)$$

Then the expected value will be:

$$NP_{rs} = \frac{P_r}{1-P_s} \cdot \frac{P_s}{1-P_r} \cdot (NP_r + NP_s)$$

For the actual computation of expected values an equivalent formula was used.

$$\frac{F_r \cdot F_s}{G_r} \cdot \frac{}{G_s} (F_r + F_s)$$

Trios.

$$P_{r,s,} = P_r \frac{P_s}{1-P_r} \cdot \frac{P_t}{1-P_s}$$

$$P_{rst} = 2 \frac{P_r}{1-P_r} \cdot \frac{P_s}{1-P_s} \cdot \frac{P_t}{1-P_t} [(1-P_r) + (1-P_s) + (1-P_t)]$$

$$NP = 2 \frac{F_r}{G_r} \cdot \frac{F_s}{G_s} \cdot \frac{F_t}{G_t} (G_r + G_s + G_t)$$

APPENDIX. NOTE (b)

The coefficient of disarray used in the study was Kendall's τ. It was used in the following way. In Table V (Appendix) the sum of deviations round the mean of members' evaluations of one another on six criteria was, for Group A:

186

week	1	2	3	4	5	6	7	8	9
	157	175	153	182	149	163	137	139	136

We count the number of scores larger than the first and to the right of it, there are three; then we count the number of scores larger than the second and to the right of it, there is one; and so on for the whole series.

$$3 \quad 1 \quad 2 \quad - \quad 1 \quad - \quad 1 \quad - \quad - \quad \text{Total 8.}$$

The formula reads:

$$\tau = \frac{2P}{\frac{1}{2}n(n-1)} - 1$$

P is the total (8)

n is the number of items (9)

$$\tau = \frac{16}{36} - 1$$

$$= -0.56$$

Where there is a regular increase in the value of numbers in a series, e.g. 1, 3, 4, 5, 8, the coefficient of disarray will be $+$ 1, where there is a decrease, the coefficient will be $-$ 1.

(M. G. Kendall, *Rank Correlation Methods*, Charles Griffin and Co., London, 1948.)

BIBLIOGRAPHY

ALLEE, W. C., *The Social Life of Animals*. Heinemann, London, 1939.

ALLPORT, F. H., *Social Psychology*. Houghton Miflin, Boston, 1924. 'The Influence of the Group upon Association and Thought', *J. Exper. Psychol*. III, 1920.

ASCH, S. E., 'Effects of Group Pressure upon the Modification and Distortion of Judgments', *in* Guetzkow, H., *edt. Groups, Leadership and Men*. Carnegie Press, Pittsburgh, 1951.

BACK, K., 'Interpersonal Relations in a Discussion Group', *J. Soc. Issues*, 1948. 'Influence through Social Communication', *J. Abn. Soc. Psychol.*, XLVI, 1951.

BACK, K., FESTINGER, L., HYMOVITCH, B., *et al.*, 'The Methodology of Rumour Transmission', *Hum. Rel.*, III, 1950.

BALES, R. F., *Interaction Process Analysis*, Addison-Wesley Press Inc., Cambridge, Mass., 1951.

BALES, R. F. and STRODTBECK, F. L., 'Phases in Group Problem Solving', *J. Abn. Soc. Psychol.*, XLVI, 1951.

BALES, R. F.; *et al.*, 'Channels of Communication in Small Groups', *Amer. Sociol. Rev.*, XVI, 1951.

BALES, R. F., PARSONS, T., and SHILS, E., *Working Papers in the Theory of Action*. The Free Press, Glencoe, Illinois, 1952.

BARNARD, C. I., *The Functions of the Executive*. Harvard Univ. Press, Cambridge, Mass., 1938.

BATES, A. P. (in Riecken and Homans, 1954).

BAVELAS, A., 'A Mathematical Model of Group Structures', *Applied Anthropology*, VII, 1948. 'Communication Patterns in Problem Solving Groups', in *Cybernetics*, edt. H. von Foerster, the transactions of the Eighth Conference. (Josiah Mason Jr. Foundation, New York), 1952.

BEKHTEREV, W. and DE LANGE, M., 'Die Ergebnisse des Experiments auf dem Gebiete der kollectiven Reflexologie', *Zsch. f. angew. Psychol.*, XXII (quoted in Dashiell infr.), 1924.

BENNE, K., and SHEATS, W., 'Functional Roles of Group Members', *J. Soc. Iss.*, IV, 1948.

BION, W. R., 'Experiences in Groups', *Hum. Rel.*, I, II, III, 1948, 1949, 1950.

BORGHATTA, E. F. and BALES, R. F., 'Interaction of Individuals in Reconstituted Groups', *Sociometry*, XVI, 1953.

BOVARD, E., 'The Experimental Production of Interpersonal Affect', *J. Abn. Soc. Psychol.*, XLVI, 1951.

'Group Structure and Perception', *ibid.*

CARTWRIGHT, D. and ZANDER, A., *Group Dynamics*. Row, Peterson and Co., Evanston, Illinois, and Tavistock Publications, London, 1953.

CHAPMAN, D. W. and VOLKMANN, J., 'A Social Determinant of the Level of Aspiration', in Newcomb, T. M., *et al. Readings in Social Psychology*. Henry Holt, New York, 1952.

CHOWDRY, K. and NEWCOMB, T. M., 'The Relative Abilities of Leaders and Non-Leaders to estimate Opinions in their own Groups', *J. Abn. Soc. Psychol.*, XLVII, 1952.

CHRISTIE, L. S., LUCE, R. B., and MACY, J., *Communication and Learning in Task-oriented Groups*. Research Laboratory of Electronics, Technical Report No. 231, Massachusetts Institute of Technology, Cambridge, Mass., 1952.

'Coding Noise in a Task-oriented Group', *J. Abn. Soc. Psychol.*, XLVIII, 1953.

COCH, L. and FRENCH, J. R. P., 'Overcoming Resistance to Change', *Hum. Rel.*, I, 1948.

COLLINS, D., DALTON, M., and ROY, D., 'Restriction of Output and Social Cleavage in Industry', *Applied Anthropology*, V., 1946.

DALTON, M., 'The Industrial Rate-buster', *Appl. Anthropology*, VII, 1948.

DASHIELL, J. F., 'An Experimental Analysis of some Group Effects', *J. Abn. Soc. Psychol.*, XXV, 1930.

'Experimental Studies of the Influence of Social Situations on the Behaviour of Individual Human Adults' (in Murchison, C., 1935).

DEUTSCH, M., 'The Effects of Co-operation and Competition upon Group Processes', *Hum. Rel.*, II (pp. 129–152 and 199–231), 1949.

DODD, S. C., 'Message Diffusion in Controlled Experiments', *Amer. Sociol. Rev.*, XVIII, 1953.

BIBLIOGRAPHY

DURKHEIM, E., *The Division of Labour in Society* (tr. Simpson, C., 1947. Free Press, Glencoe; Allen and Unwin, London) 1893. *Sociology and Philosophy* (tr. Pocock, D. F., 1953). Cohen and West, London, 1898.

FESTINGER, L., 'Group Belongingness in a Voting Situation', *Hum. Rel.*, I, 1947.

FESTINGER, L. and CARTWRIGHT, D., *et al.*, 'A Study of Rumour; its Origin and Spread', *Hum. Rel.*, I, 1948.

FESTINGER, L., SCHACHTER, S., and BACH, K., *Social Pressures in Informal Groups*. Harper, New York, 1950.

FESTINGER, L., GERARD, *et al.*, 'The Influence Process in the Presence of Extreme Deviates', *Hum. Rel.*, V, 1952.

FESTINGER, L., 'A Theory of Social Comparison Processes', *Hum. Rel.*, VII, 1954.

FOLLETT, M. P., *Freedom and Co-ordination*, edt. Urwick, Management Publication Trust, London, 1949.

FRENCH, J. R. P., 'Organised and Unorganised Groups under Fear and Frustration', *Univ. Iowa Stud. Child Welf.*, XX, no. 409, 1944.

FREUD, S., *Group Psychology and the Analysis of the Ego*. Internat. Psycho-analytical Library (tr. J. Strachey, 1949, Hogarth, London) 1921.

FROMM, E., *The Fear of Freedom*. Kegan Paul, London, 1942.

GIBB, C. A., 'The Sociometry of Leadership', *Sociometry*, XIII, 1950.

GILCHRIST, J. C., 'Social Groups under Conditions of Success and Failure', *J. Abn. Soc. Psychol.*, XLVII, 1952.

GOLDMAN-EISLER, F., 'The Measurement of Time-sequences in Conversational Behaviour', *Brit. J. Psychol.*, XLII, 1951.

GORDON, K., 'Group Judgments in the Field of Lifted Weights', *J. Exper. Psychol.*, VII, 1924.

GROSS, N., MARTIN, W., and DARLEY, J. G., 'Leadership Structures in small Organised Groups', *J. Abn. Soc. Psychol.*, XLVIII, 1953.

GUETZKOW, H. (edt.), *Groups, Leadership and Men*. Carnegie Press, Pittsburgh, 1951.

GURNEE, H., 'Maze Learning in the Collective Situation', *J. Psychol.*, III, 1937.

HANFMAN, E., 'Social Structure of a Kindergarten Group', *Amer. J. Orthopsychiatry*, V., 1938.

191

THE STUDY OF GROUPS

HARE, A. P., 'Interaction and Consensus in different-sized Groups', *Amer. Sociol. Rev.*, XVII (also in Cartwright and Zander, *op. cit.*), 1952.

HARRIS, H., *The Group Approach to Leadership Testing*. Routledge and Kegan Paul, London, 1949.

HARVEY, O. J., 'Status Relations in Informal Groups', *Amer. Sociol. Rev.*, VIII, 1953.

HEINECKE, C., and BALES, R. F., 'Developmental Trends in the Structure of Small Groups', *Sociometry*, XVI, 1953.

HEISE, G. A. and MILLER, G. A., 'Problem Solving by Small Groups using various Communication Nets', *J. Abn. Soc. Psychol.*, XLVI, 1951.

HEMPHILL, J. K., 'Relations between Size of Groups and the Behaviour of "Superior" Leaders', *J. Soc. Psychol.*, XXXII, 1950.

HOMANS, G. C., *The Human Group*. Harcourt, Brace and Co. Inc., New York; Routledge and Kegan Paul, London, 1950.

HUGHES, E. C., 'The Knitting of Racial Groups in Industry', *Amer. Sociol. Rev.*, XI, 1946.

HURLOCK, E. B., 'The Use of Group Rivalry as an Incentive', *J. Abn. Soc. Psychol.*, XXII, 1927.

HURWITZ, J. I., ZANDER, A., and HYMOVITCH, B., 'Some Effects of Power on the Relations among Group Members' (in Cartwright and Zander, *op. cit.*), 1953.

HUSBAND, R. W., 'Co-operative versus Solitary Problem-solution', *J. Soc. Psychol.*, XI., 1940.

JENNESS, A., 'Social Influences in the Change of Opinion', *J. Abn. Soc. Psychol.*, XXVII, 1932.

JENNINGS, H. H., *Leadership and Isolation* (second edition), Longmans, Green, New York, 1950.
'Sociometric Differentiation of the Psychegroup and the Sociogroup', *Sociometry*, X, 1947.

KELLEY, H. H., 'Communication in Experimentally created Hierarchies', *Hum. Rel.*, IV, 1951.

KENDALL, M. G., *Rank Correlation Methods*. Griffin and Co., London, 1948.

KEPHART, W. M., 'Quantitative Analysis of Intra-group Relationships', *Amer. J. Sociol.*, LV, 1949, 1950.

LASSWELL, H. D. and KAPLAN, A., *Power and Society*. Routledge and Kegan Paul, London; Yale U.P., Newhaven, 1950.

BIBLIOGRAPHY

LEAVITT, H. J., 'Some Effects of certain Communication Patterns on Group Performance', *J. Abn. Soc. Psychol.*, XLVI, 1951.

LEEMAN, C. P., 'Patterns of Sociometric Choice in Small Groups', *Sociometry*, XV., 1952.

LEWIN, K., *Field Theory in Social Science*. Tavistock Publications, London; Harper, New York, 1952.

LEWIN, K., LIPPITT, R., and WHITE, R. K., 'Patterns of aggressive Behaviour in experimentally created social Climates', *J. Soc. Psychol.*, X, 1939.

LIPPITT, R., 'The Effect of Democratic and Authoritarian Group Atmospheres', *Univ. Iowa Stud. in Child Welf*, no. 16, 1940.

LORENZ, E., 'Zur Psychologie der industriellen Gruppenarbeit', *Zsch. f. angew. Psychol.*, XLV. 1933 (see also Dashiell, 1930, *op. cit.*).

MCCURDY, H. G. and LAMBERT, W. E., 'The Efficiency of Small Human Groups in the Solution of Problems requiring Genuine Co-operation', *J. Personality*, XX, 1952.

MCCURDY, H. G. and EBER, H. W., 'A further Investigation of Group Problem Solving', *J. Personality*, XXI, 1953.

MAIER, N. R. F., 'The Quality of Group Discussion as influenced by a Discussion Leader', *Hum. Rel.*, III, 1950.

MAIER, N. R. F. and SOLEM, A. R., 'The Contribution of a Discussion Leader to the Quality of Group Thinking', *Hum. Rel.*, V, 1952.

MEREI, F., 'Group Leadership and Institutionalisation', *Hum. Rel.*, II, 1949.

MINTZ, A., 'Non-adaptive Group Behaviour', *J. Abn. Soc. Psychol.*, XLVI, 1951.

MILLER, J. G., *Experiments in Social Process*. McGraw Hill, New York, 1950.

MILLS, T. M., 'Power Relations in Three Person Groups', *Amer. Sociol. Rev.*, XVIII, 1953.

MOEDE, W., *Experimentelle Massenpsychologie*. Hirzel, Leipzig, 1920. 'Die Richtlinien der Leistungspsychologie', *Indus. Psychotech.*, IV, 1927 (see also Dashiell, *op. cit.*).

MORENO, J. L., *Who Shall Survive?* Beacon House, Beacon, New York, 1934.

MURCHISON, C., 'The Formation of Social Hierarchies in *Gallus Domesticus*'. A series of articles in *J. General Psychol.*, VII, *J. Genetic Psychol.*, VI, and *J. Soc. Psychol.*, V, 1934–5.

Handbook in Social Psychology. Clark U.P., Worcester, Mass., 1935.

WCOMB, T. M., 'Autistic Hostility and Social Reality', *Hum. Rel.*, I, 1947, 1948.

FLEET, B., 'Interpersonal and Group Productivity', *J. Soc. Iss.*, IV, 1948.

NOWLIS, V., 'Companionship Preferences and Dominance in Social Interaction', *Comp. Psychol. Monog.*, XVII, 1939.

OGBURN, W. F. and NIMKOFF, M. F., *A Handbook of Sociology*. Kegan Paul, London, 1947.

PARSONS, T., BALES, R. F., and SHILS, E., *Working Papers in the Theory of Action*. Free Press, Glencoe, Illinois, 1953.

PENROSE, L. S., *On the Objective Study of Crowd Behaviour*. H. K. Lewis and Co., London, 1952.

PEPITONE, A., 'Motivational Effects on Social Perception', *Hum. Rel.*, III, 1950.

POLANSKY, N., LIPPITT, R., and REDL, F., 'Behavioural Contagion in Groups', *Hum. Rel.*, III, 1950.

RIECKEN, H. W. and HOMANS, G. C., 'Psychological Aspects of Social Structure', in Lindzey, G. (edt.) *Handbook of Social Psychology*. Cambridge, Mass. 1954.

ROGERS, C., *Client-centred Therapy*. Houghton Mifflin, Boston, 1951.

ROY, D., 'Goal Breaking and Quota Restriction', *Amer. J. Sociol.*, LVII, 1952.

SCHACHTER, S., 'Deviation, Rejection and Communication', *J. Abn. Soc. Psychol.*, XLVI, 1951.

SCHJELDERUP-EBBE, T., 'Fortgesetzte biologische Beobachtungen des *Gallus Domesticus*', *Psychol. Forsch.*, V, 1924 (see also Dashiell in Murchison, *op. cit.*).

SENGUPTA, N. N. and SINHA, C. P. N., 'Mental Work in Isolation and in Groups', *Indian J. Psychol.*, I, 1926.

SHAW, M. E., 'A Comparison of Individuals and Small Groups in the rational Solution of complex Problems', *J. Abn. Soc. Psychol.*, XLIV, 1938.

SHERIF, M., *The Psychology of Social Norms*. Harper, New York, 1936.

'A preliminary Study of Inter-group Relations', in Rohrer, J. H., and Sherif, M., *Social Psychology at the Crossroads*. Harper, New York, 1951.

BIBLIOGRAPHY

SIMON, H. A., *Administrative Behaviour*. MacMillan, New York, 1947.
'A formal Theory of Interaction in Groups', *Amer. Sociol. Rev.*, XVII, 1952.
'A Comparison of Organisation Theories', *Rev. Econ. Stud.*, XX, 1952.

SOUTH, E. B., 'Some psychological Aspects of Committee Work', *J. Applied Psychol.*, XI, 1927.

SPROTT, W. H. J., *Social Psychology*. Methuen, London, 1952.

STROOP, J. R., 'Is the judgement of the Group better than that of the average Member?' *J. Exper. Psychol.*, XV, 1932.

STRODTBECK, F. L., 'Husband-Wife Interaction over revealed Differences', *Amer. Sociol. Rev.*, XVI, 1951.

THIBAUT, J., 'An experimental Study of the Cohesiveness of underprivileged Groups', *Hum. Rel.*, III, 1950.

THOMPSON, J. and NISHIMURA, R., 'Some Determinants of Friendship', *J. Personality*, XX, 1951-2.

THORNDIKE, R. L., 'On what Type of Task will a Group do well', *J. Abn. Soc. Psychol.*, XXXIII, 1938.

THURSTONE, L. L. and CHAVE, E. J., *The Measurement of Attitude*. Chicago U.P., 1932.

TRAVIS, L. E., 'The Effect of a Small Audience on Hand-Eye Coordination', *J. Abn. Soc. Psychol.*, XX, 1925.

WATSON, G. B., 'Do groups think more efficiently than Individuals?' *J. Abn. Soc. Psychol.*, XXIII, 1928.

WHITTEMORE, I. C., 'Influence of Competition on Performance', *J. Abn. Soc. Psychol.*, XIX, 1924.
'The Competition Consciousness', *ibid.*, XX, 1925.

WHYTE, W. F., *Street Corner Society*. Univ. Chicago Press, 1943.

Index